AF255897

Climbing a Few of Japan's 100 Famous Mountains –
Volume 3:
Mt. Gassan

Daniel H. Wieczorek and Kazuya Numazawa

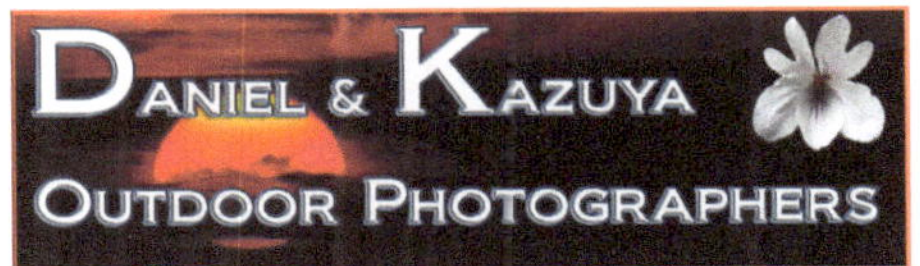

Climbing a Few of Japan's 100 Famous Mountains –
Volume 3:
Mt. Gassan

Rev. 1

DEDICATION

This work is dedicated, first of all, to my partner, Kazuya Numazawa. He always keeps my interest in photography up and makes me keep striving for the perfect photo. He also often makes me think of the expression "when the going gets tough, the tough keep going." Without my partner it has to also be noted that I most likely would not have climbed any of these mountains.

Secondly, it is dedicated to my mother and father, bless them, for tolerating and even encouraging my photography hobby from the time I was twelve years old.

And, finally, it is dedicated to my friends who have encouraged me to create books of photographs which I have taken while doing mountain climbing.

Other Books in this Series

"Climbing a Few of Japan's 100 Famous Mountains – Volume 1: Mt. Daisetsu (Mt. Asahidake)"; ISBN-13: 9781493777204; 66 Pages; Dec. 5, 2013

"Climbing a Few of Japan's 100 Famous Mountains – Volume 2: Mt. Chokai (Choukai)"; ISBN-13: 9781494368401; 72 Pages; Dec. 8, 2013

"Climbing a Few of Japan's 100 Famous Mountains – Volume 4: Mt. Hakkoda & Mt. Zao"; ISBN-13: 9781495396564; 88 Pages; Jan. 31, 2014

"Climbing a Few of Japan's 100 Famous Mountains – Volume 5: Mt. Kumotori"; ISBN-13: 9781495980527; 84 Pages; February 17, 2014

"A Pocket-Size Version of Climbing a Few of Japan's 100 Famous Mountains – Volume 5: Mt. Kumotori"; ISBN-13: 9781497444942; 90 Pages; March 25, 2014

"Climbing a Few of Japan's 100 Famous Mountains – Volume 6: Mt. Shirane (Kusatsu)"; ISBN-13: 9781497303232; 80 Pages; March 11, 2014

"Climbing a Few of Japan's 100 Famous Mountains – Volume 7: Mt. Shibutsu"; ISBN-13: 9781497539273; 80 Pages; April 4, 2014

"Climbing a Few of Japan's 100 Famous Mountains – Volume 8: Mt. Kiso-Komagatake"; ISBN-13: 9781499178630; 72 Pages; April 18, 2014

"Climbing a Few of Japan's 100 Famous Mountains – Volume 9: Mt. Kitadake"; ISBN-13: 9781499786088; 62 Pages; June 4, 2014

"Climbing a Few of Japan's 100 Famous Mountains – Volume 10: Mt. Mizugaki"; ISBN-13: 9781500235284; 70 Pages; June 18, 2014

"Climbing a Few of Japan's 100 Famous Mountains – Volume 11: Mt. Shiroumadake (includes Mt. Shakushidake & Mt. Yarigatake)"; ISBN-13: 9781500463885; 178 Pages; July 9, 2014

"Climbing a Few of Japan's 100 Famous Mountains – Volume 12: Mt. Tate (Tateyama)"; ISBN-13: 9781500946326; 176 Pages; Aug. 26, 2014

"Climbing a Few of Japan's 100 Famous Mountains – Volume 13: Mt. Yatsugatake (Mt. Akadake)"; ISBN-13: 9781502877581; 208 Pages; October 22, 2014

FOREWORD

What is the purpose of this series of books? It is to show you, in photographs, some of the astounding sights and scenery we have seen while climbing the mountains included herein. At this time we have climbed 14 of Japan's 100 Famous Mountains. The ones we have climbed are: 1) Mt. Daisetsu (2,290 m) (大雪山) = Mt. Asahidake (旭岳); 2) Mt. Chokai (2,236 m) (鳥海山); 3) Mt. Gassan (1,984 m) (月山); 4) Mt. Hakkoda (1,584 m) (八甲田山); 5) Mt. Zao (1,841 m) (蔵王山); 6) Mt. Kumotori (2,017 m) (雲取山); 7) Mt. Kusatsu-Shirane (2,171 m) (草津白根山); 8) Mt. Shibutsu (2,228 m) (至仏山); 9) Mt. Kiso-Komagatake (2,956 m) (木曾駒ヶ岳); 10) Mt. Kitadake (North Peak) (3,192 m) (北岳); 11) Mt. Mizugaki (2,230 m) (瑞牆山); 12) Mt. Shiroumadake (2,932 m) (白馬岳); 13) Mt. Tateyama (3,015 m) (立山); and 14) Mt. Yatsugatake (2,899 m) (八ヶ岳).

By the way, I (Daniel) did all of the writing and Kazuya did a fair percentage of the photography. So, do not be surprised from time to time when you see references such as "Kazuya" and "that's me…".

Daniel and Kazuya's ***"Outdoor Photography of Japan: Through the Seasons"*** includes some of the same photos as this work, but this work may be thought of as a subset of that work because that work includes adventures to many mountains beyond the 14 famous mountains which are found in this series of books. In addition, the photos in that book were more than 50% flower photos. This series includes less than 1% flower photos, and only where the flower is a part of a mountain scene. In addition, the majority of the photos you'll find in this series were not included in that work.

TABLE OF CONTENTS

Regions & Prefectures of Japan

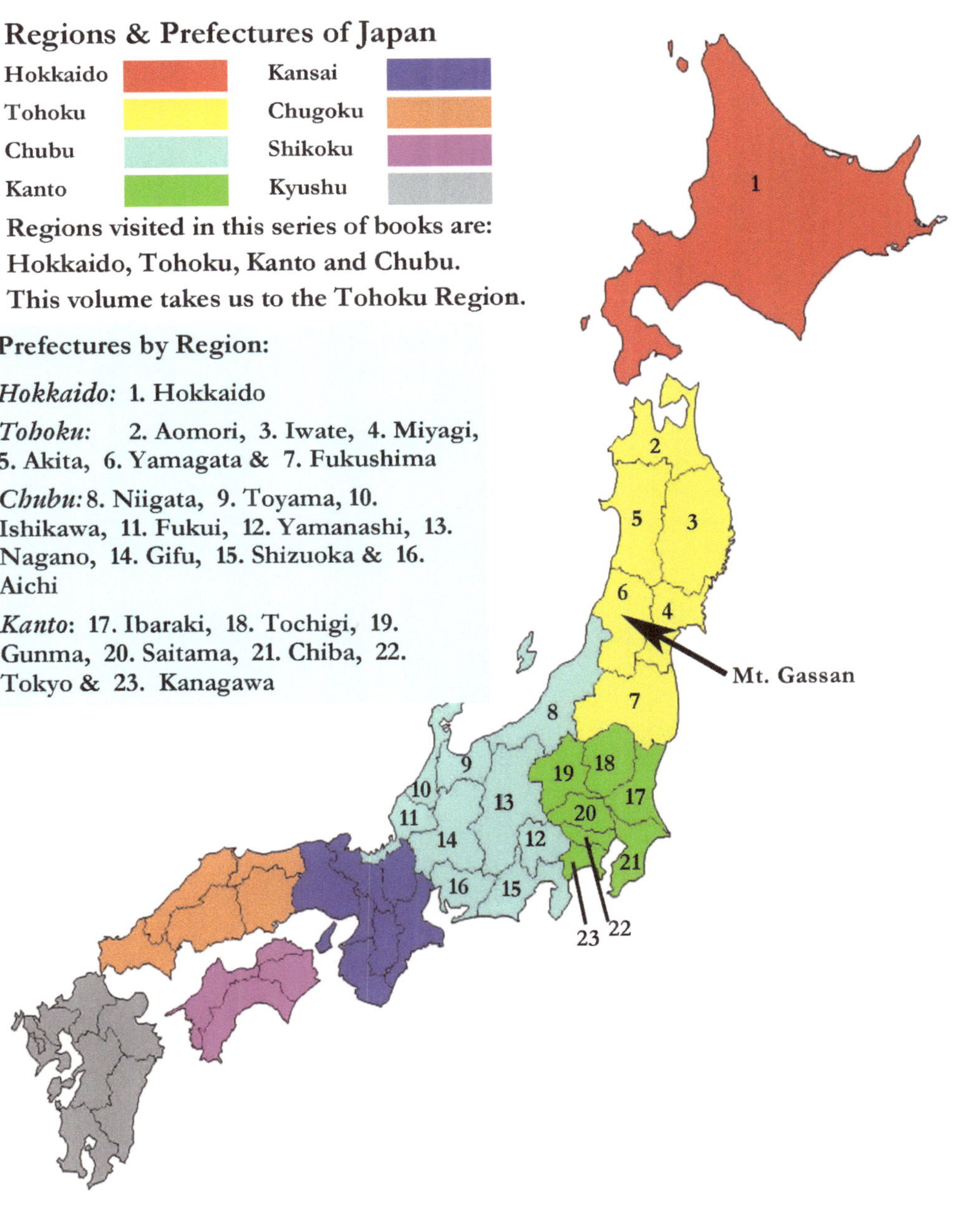

Regions visited in this series of books are:
Hokkaido, Tohoku, Kanto and Chubu.
This volume takes us to the Tohoku Region.

Prefectures by Region:

Hokkaido: 1. Hokkaido

Tohoku: 2. Aomori, 3. Iwate, 4. Miyagi, 5. Akita, 6. Yamagata & 7. Fukushima

Chubu: 8. Niigata, 9. Toyama, 10. Ishikawa, 11. Fukui, 12. Yamanashi, 13. Nagano, 14. Gifu, 15. Shizuoka & 16. Aichi

Kanto: 17. Ibaraki, 18. Tochigi, 19. Gunma, 20. Saitama, 21. Chiba, 22. Tokyo & 23. Kanagawa

1) JAPAN'S 100 FAMOUS MOUNTAINS

What are Japan's 100 famous mountains? A selection of famous mountains in Japan has been compiled since the Edo period (1603 – 1867) and the list has been revised several times since the very first list appeared. At the current time the list of 100 famous mountains includes those shown below. Also shown is the Japanese pronunciation, elevation in meters and feet, the Japanese kanji, the Region the mountain is in and a few a.k.a. (also known as) names.

Hokkaido:

1.	Mt. Akan (Akandake)	1,499	4,918	阿寒岳
2.	**Mt. Asahi (Asahidake) a.k.a.**			
	Mt. Daisetsu (Daisetsuzan)	**2,290**	**7,513**	**旭岳**
	a.k.a. (大雪山)			
3.	Mt. Poroshiri (Poroshiridake)	2,052	6,734	幌尻岳
4.	Mt. Rausu (Rausudake)	1,660	5,446	羅臼岳
5.	Mt. Rishiri (Rishiridake)	1,721	5,646	利尻岳
6.	Mt. Shari (Sharidake)	1,545	5,069	斜里岳
7.	Mt. Tokachi (Tochidake)	2,077	6,814	十勝岳
8.	Mt. Tomuraushi (Tomuraushiyama)	2,141	7,024	
	トムラウシ山			
9.	Mt. Yotei (Yoteizan) a.k.a.			
	(Mt. Shiribeshi) (Shiribeshiyama)	1,893	6,211	羊蹄山
	a.k.a. (後方羊蹄山)			

Tohoku Region:

10.	Mt. Adatara (Adatarayama)	1,700	5,577	
	安達太良山			
11.	Mt. Aizu-Komagatake (Aizukomagatake)			
		2,132	6,995	会津駒ケ岳
12.	Mt. Asahi (Asahirenpou)	1,870	6,135	朝日連峰
13.	Mt. Azuma (Azumayama)	2,035	6,676	吾妻山
14.	Mt. Bandai (Bandaisan)	1,819	5,968	磐梯山
15.	**Mt. Chōkai (Chōkaisan)**	**2,236**	**7,336**	**鳥海山**
16.	**Mt. Gassan (Gassan)**	**1,984**	**6,509**	**月山**
17.	Mt. Hachimantai (Hachimantai)	1,614	5,295	八幡平
18.	**Mt. Hakkōda (Hakkōdasan)**	**1,584**	**5,197**	**八甲田山**

19.	Mt. Hayachine (Hayachinesan)	1,917	6,289	早池峰山
20.	Mt. Hiuchigatake (Hiuchigatake)	2,356	7,730	燧ケ岳
21.	Mt. Iide (Iiderenpou)	2,105	6,906	飯豊連峰
22.	Mt. Iwaki (Iwakisan)	1,625	5,331	岩木山
23.	Mt. Iwate (Iwatesan)	2,038	6,686	岩手山
24.	**Mt. Zaō (Zaōsan)**	**1,841**	**6,040**	**蔵王山**

Kanto Region:

25.	Mt. Akagi (Akagiyama)	1,828	5,997	赤城山
26.	Mt. Asama (Asamayama)	2,568	8,425	浅間山
27.	Mt. Azumaya (Azumayasan)	2,354	7,723	四阿山
28.	Mt. Hiragatake (Hiragatake)	2,141	7,024	平ヶ岳
29.	Mt. Hotaka (Hotakayama)	2,158	7,080	武尊山
30.	**Mt. Kumotori (Kumotoriyama)**	**2,017**	**6,617**	**雲取山**
31.	**Mt. Kusatsu-Shirane (Kusatsu-Shiranesan)**	**2,171**	**7,123**	**草津白根山**
32.	Mt. Nantai (Nantaisan)	2,486	8,156	男体山
33.	Mt. Nasu (Nasudake)	1,915	6,283	那須岳
34.	Mt. Nikko-Shirane (Nikko-Shiranesan)	2,578	8,458	日光白根山
35.	Mt. Ryokami (Ryoukamisan)	1,723	5,653	両神山
36.	**Mt. Shibutsu (Shibutsusan)**	**2,228**	**7,310**	**至仏山**
37.	Mt. Sukai (Sukaisan)	2,144	7,034	皇海山
38.	Mt. Tanigawa (Tanigawadake)	1,963	6,440	谷川岳
39.	Mt. Tanzawa (Tanzawasan)	1,567	5,141	丹沢山
40.	Mt. Tsukuba (Tsukubasan)	877	2,877	筑波山

Chubu Region:

41.	Mt. Ainodake (Ainodake)	3,189	10,463	間ノ岳
42.	Mt. Akaishi (Akaishidake)	3,120	10,236	赤石岳
43.	Mt. Amagi (Amagisan)	1,406	4,613	天城山
44.	Mt. Amakazari (Amakazariyama)	1,963	6,440	雨飾山
45.	Mt. Daibosatsu (Daibosatsurei)	2,057	6,749	大菩薩嶺
46.	Mt. Ena (Enasan)	2,191	7,188	恵那山
47.	Mt. Fuji (Fujisan)	3,776	12,388	富士山
48.	Mt. Goryū (Goryūdake)	2,814	9,232	五竜岳
49.	Mt. Hakusan (Hakusan)	2,702	8,865	白山
50.	Mt. Hijiri (Hijiridake)	3,013	9,885	聖岳
51.	Mt. Hiuchi (Hiuchiyama)	2,462	8,077	火打山
52.	Mt. Hōō (Hōōsan)	2,840	9,318	鳳凰山

53.	Mt. Hotaka (Hotakadake)	3,190	10,466	穂高岳
54.	Mt. Jōnen (Jōnendake)	2,857	9,373	常念岳
55.	Mt. Kai-Komagatake (Kaikomagatake)	2,967	9,734	甲斐駒ケ岳
56.	Mt. Kasa (Kasagatake)	2,897	9,505	笠ヶ岳
57.	Mt. Kashima Yarigatake (Kashimayarigatake)			
		2,889	9,478	鹿島槍ヶ岳
58.	Mt. Kinpu (Kinpusan)	2,599	8,527	金峰山
59.	Mt. Kirigamine (Kirigamine)	1,925	6,316	霧ヶ峰
60.	**Mt. Kiso-Komagatake (Kisokomagatake)**			
		2,956	**9,698**	**木曽駒ケ岳**
61.	**Mt. Kitadake (Kitadake)**	**3,192**	**10,472**	**北岳**
62.	Mt. Kobushi (Kobushidake)	2,475	8,120	甲武信岳
63.	Mt. Kuro (Kurodake) a.k.a.			
	(Mt. Suisho) (Suishodake)	2,978	9,770	黒岳
	a.k.a. (水晶岳)			
64.	Mt. Kurobe-Gorō (Kurobegorōdake)	2,840	9,318	黒部五郎岳
65.	Mt. Makihata (Makihatayama)	1,967	6,453	巻機山
66.	**Mt. Mizugaki (Mizugakiyama)**	**2,230**	**7,316**	**瑞牆山**
67.	Mt. Myoko (Myokosan)	2,454	8,051	妙高山
68.	Mt. Naeba (Naebasan)	2,145	7,037	苗場山
69.	Mt. Norikura (Norikuradake)	3,026	9,928	乗鞍岳
70.	Mt. Ontake (Ontakesan)	3,067	10,062	御嶽山
71.	Mt. Senjōgatake (Senjōgatake)	3,033	9,951	仙丈ケ岳
72.	Mt. Shiomi (Shiomidake)	3,047	9,997	塩見岳
73.	**Mt. Shiroumadake (Shiroumadake)**	**2,932**	**9,619**	**白馬岳**
74.	Mt. Takatsuma (Takatsumayama)	2,353	7,720	高妻山
75.	Mt. Tateshina (Tateshinayama)	2,530	8,301	蓼科山
76.	**Mt. Tateyama (Tateyama)**	**3,015**	**9,892**	**立山**
77.	Mt. Tekari (Tekaridake)	2,591	8,501	光岳
78.	Mt. Tsurugi (Tsurugidake)	2,999	9,839	剱岳
79.	Mt. Uonuma-Komagatake a.k.a.			
	(Echigo-Komagatake)	2,003	6,572	魚沼駒ヶ岳
	a.k.a. (越後駒ケ岳)			
80.	Mt. Utsugi (Utsugidake)	2,864	9,396	空木岳
81.	Mt. Warusawa (Warusawadake)	3,141	10,305	悪沢岳
82.	Mt. Washiba (Washibadake)	2,924	9,593	鷲羽岳
83.	Mt. Yake (Yakedake)	2,444	8,018	焼岳

84.	Mt. Yakushi (Yakushidake)	2,926	9,600	薬師岳
85.	Mt. Yarigatake (Yarigatake)	3,180	10,433	槍ヶ岳
86.	**Mt. Yatsugatake (Yatsugatake)**	**2,899**	**9,511**	**八ヶ岳**
87.	Utsukushigahara Highland (Utsukushigahara)	2,034	6,673	美ヶ原

Western Japan:

88.	Mt. Arashima (Arashimadake)	1,523	4,997	荒島岳
89.	Mt. Aso (Asosan)	1,592	5,223	阿蘇山
90.	Mt. Daisen (Daisen)	1,729	5,673	大山
91.	Mt. Ibuki (Ibukiyama)	1,377	4,518	伊吹山
92.	Mt. Ishizuchi (Ishizuchisan)	1,982	6,503	石鎚山
93.	Mt. Kaimon (Kaimondake)	924	3,031	開聞岳
94.	Mt. Kirishima (Kirishimayama)	1,700	5,577	霧島山
95.	Mt. Kujū (Kujūsan)	1,791	5,876	九重山
96.	Mt. Miya-no-ura (Miyanouradake)	1,936	6,352	宮之浦岳
97.	Mt. Ōmine (Ōminesan)	1,915	6,283	大峰山
98.	Mt. Sobo (Sobosan)	1,756	5,761	祖母山
99.	Mt. Tsurugi (Tsurugisan)	1,955	6,414	剣山
100.	The Wide Mountain of Ōdai (Ōdaigaharayama)	1,695	5,561	大台ケ原山

My partner and I have climbed (or in one, case merely ascended) the fourteen mountains which are **shaded, underlined and in bold** text. You'll probably note that we have not climbed Mt. Fuji and wonder why? The reason is simple – too many people and not enough interesting sights.

Using photographs and a minimum amount of text we are telling (showing) you the stories of climbing the 14 mountains shown above. We started at the beginning of the 100 mountains list and are working our way through it. That means that the first climb we showed you, in Volume 1, was on Hokkaido and it was a climb of Mt. Daisetsu (2,290.9 m = 7,516 ft) (大雪山), which is also known as Mt. Asahidake. Mt. Daisetsu is the name of the entire mountain range, while Mount Asahi (旭岳 Asahidake) is the tallest mountain in that mountain range and also the tallest mountain in Hokkaido Prefecture, Japan. It is part of the Daisetsuzan Volcanic Group and it is located in the northern part of Daisetsuzan National Park.

The second mountain we showed you, in Volume 2, was in the Tohoku Region and the mountain name was Mt. Chokai (or Choukai) (2,236 m = 7,336 ft) (鳥海山). Mt. Chokai is located on the southern border of Akita Prefecture and the northern border of Yamagata Prefecture. It is still an active volcano and it is the second tallest mountain in the Tohoku Region of Japan.

The third mountain we'll show you – in this volume – is also in the Tohoku Region and it is Mt. Gassan (1,984 m = 6,509 ft) (月山). Mt. Gassan is the highest peak in the Dewa Sanzan trio of sacred mountains. It lies between Mt. Chokai to the north, and Mt. Asahi to the south, in Yamagata Prefecture. Being a sacred mountain, it is famous for the shrine at the summit and in the summer you can often see large groups of white-clothed pilgrims hiking to or from the summit.

The fourth mountain we will show you is also in the Tohoku Region of Japan and the mountain will be Mt. Hakkoda (1,584 m = 5,197 ft) (八甲田山). The Hakkoda Mountains are a volcanic mountain range that lie south of Aomori City, in Aomori Prefecture Japan. The peak name is actually Mt. Hakkoda – Odake. Odake is the tallest peak in the Hakkoda Range.

The fifth mountain we'll show you is Mt. Zao (1,841 m = 6,040 ft) (蔵王山). It is also in the Tohoku Region and also in Yamagata Prefecture. We did not actually make it to the summit of this mountain. We visited it in the winter and it was very cold and windy. We took an automobile as far as possible and then transferred to a gondola car and went only a little bit beyond the top of the gondola – to about the 1,661 m (= 5,449 ft) level of the mountain. We do, however, have some impressive photos from that trip.

The sixth mountain you'll see in this series of books will be Mt. Kumotori (2,017.7 m = 6,620 ft) (雲取山). This is in the Kanto Region and the peak divides the prefectures of Tokyo, Yamanashi and Saitama. Its summit is the highest point in Tokyo. It separates the Okutama Mountains and the Okuchichibu Mountains. No matter which direction you choose to come to this mountain from, the summit is a long hike from the nearest bus stop, road end or train station.

The seventh mountain will be Mt. Kusatsu-Shirane (2,171 m = 7,123 ft) (草津白根山). This peak is also in the Kanto Region of Japan, in Gunma Prefecture. It is called Mt. Kusatsu-Shirane to differentiate it from Mt. Nikko-Shirane, which is on the opposite side of Gunma Prefecture. There is a beautifully colored volcanic pond here known as Yugama. Another volcanic pond close-by is Yumiike and there is a dry crater named Karagama Crater.

The eighth mountain, also in the Kanto Region, in Gunma Prefecture, will be Mt. Shibutsu (2,228 m = 7,310 ft) (至仏山). It separates Oze Marsh (Oze National Park) from the remainder of Gunma Prefecture. It is an interesting mountain composed primarily of serpentinite. There is also a lesser peak known as Mt. Koshibutsu (2,162 m = 7,093 ft).

The ninth mountain we'll take you to is Mt. Kiso-Komagatake (2,956 m = 9,698 ft) (木曾駒ヶ岳). It can be found in Nagano Prefecture, in the Chubu Region. It is located in Japan's Central Alps Mountain Range and is the highest peak in that range.

Then we'll very briefly take you to the tenth of Japan's 100 famous mountains which we have climbed – Mt. Kitadake (North Peak) (3,193 m = 10,476 ft) (北岳). This is Japan's second highest mountain after Mt. Fuji and is known as "the Leader of the Southern Alps". It is in Yamanashi Prefecture, in the Chubu Region.

Mt. Mizugaki (2,230 m = 7,317 ft) (瑞牆山) is the eleventh mountain that will be addressed in this series of books. It too is in the Chubu Region. It is in Yamanashi Prefecture. It lies across the valley from the Southern Alps, slightly southeast of Yatsugatake and northwest of the Daibosatsu ridgeline. Granite towers, blocks and obelisks protrude from the summit of this mountains. It is truly an amazing sight to see from its lower slopes.

Then we'll continue on to the twelfth mountain and that is also in the Chubu Region. It is Mt. Shiroumadake (2,932 m = 9,620 ft) (白馬岳). It is the tallest peak in the Hakuba section of the Hida Mountains, also known as Japan's Northern Alps Mountain Range. It is in Nagano Prefecture.

After that, for the thirteenth mountain, we'll take you to another Chubu Region mountain – Mt. Tateyama (3,015 m = 9,892 ft) (立山). It can be found in the southeastern portion of Toyama Prefecture and it also is a mountain in the Northern Alps Mountain Range, or Hida Mountains. It is one of the tallest peaks in the Hida Mountains and is the highest peak in Toyama Prefecture.

The fourteenth and final mountain we'll cover in this series of books is also in the Chubu Region – Mt. Yatsugatake (Mt. Akadake – 2,899 m = 9,511 ft) (八ヶ岳). Yatsugatake means "eight peaks" and the highest mountain in this range is Mt. Akadake. Actually there are many more than eight peaks, but in Japanese the kanji character for Hachi (八) sometimes implies "many" or "several.

According to legend, Yatsugatake was once higher than Mount Fuji, but Konohana-Sakuyahime, the goddess of Mount Fuji, tore it down out of jealousy, leaving the collection of peaks we have today. This could possibly be true considering that Yatsugatake is older than Fuji and as Fuji rose in prominence Yatsugatake wore away.

Another version of this legend says that a long time ago, Yatsugatake was an ordinary mountain with only one peak, and it was as high as or higher then Mt. Fuji. Yatsugatake's god and Mt. Fuji's goddess began quarreling over their height. Each of them insisted that he/she was taller. The Amitabha Buddha, who was entrusted to arbitrate the dispute, set a valley between the tops of the two mountains and filled it with water. The water submerged the summit of Mt. Fuji, revealing that Yatsugatake was indeed, taller. Mt. Fuji's goddess, who was unyielding, was very angry so she kept striking Yatsugatake with a long stick until it was divided into several peaks, all lower than Mt. Fuji. That is why Mt. Yatsugatake now has so many peaks. Interesting!

By the way – *dake* or *take* (岳) = peak or high peak. Some authors prefer to leave this term off when referring to a Japanese mountain, for example they will refer to Mt. Kitadake as Mt. Kita and use the argument that it is redundant to use the –dake portion of the name. We prefer to use the dake suffix for completeness. If one is to be absolutely correct it should probably be called Kita Peak, not Mt. Kita.

"Mountains are the cathedrals where I practice my religion."
— Anatoli Boukreev

*"Climb the mountains and get their good tidings. Nature's peace
will flow into you as sunshine flows into trees. The winds will blow
their own freshness into you, and the storms their energy, while cares
will drop away from you like the leaves of Autumn."*
— John Muir, The Mountains of California

"Chasing angels or fleeing demons, go to the mountains."
— Jeffrey Rasley

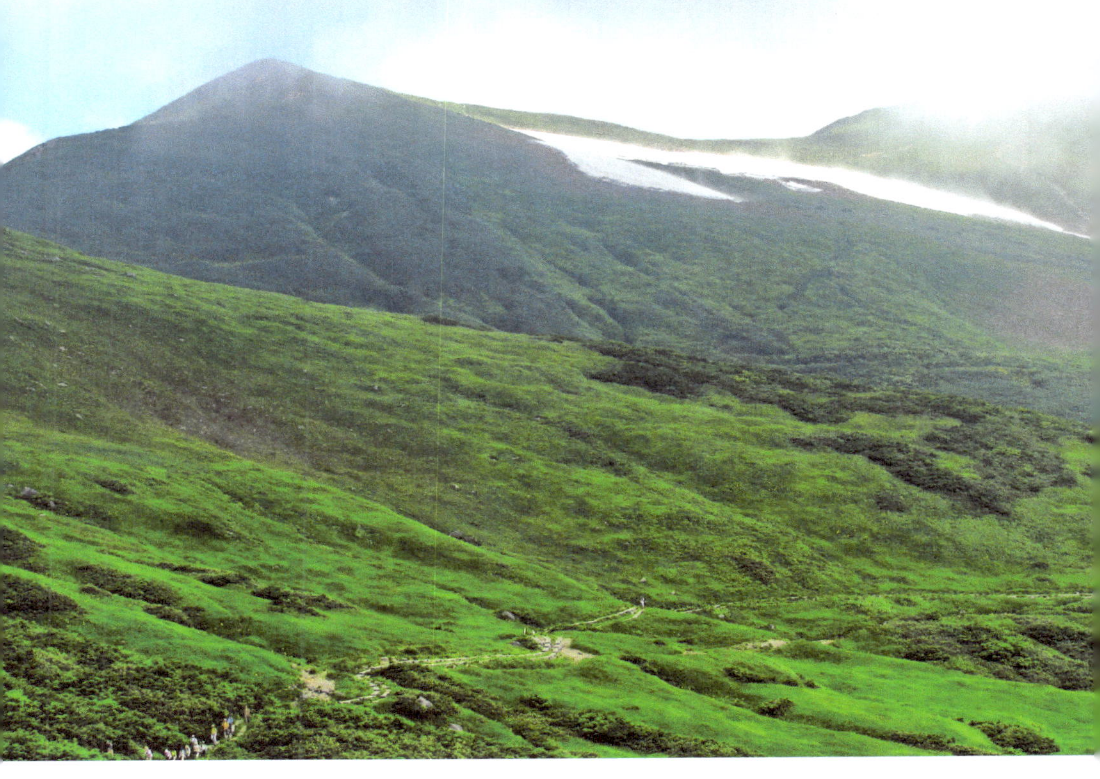

2) Mt. Gassan

This is the third climb that we are showing you in this series of books. It is a climb of Mt. Gassan (1,984 m = 6,509 ft) (月山). Mt. Gassan is the highest peak in the Dewa Sanzan trio of sacred mountains. It lies between Mt. Chokai to the north, and Mt. Asahi to the south, in Yamagata Prefecture. Being a sacred mountain, it is famous for the shrine at the summit and in the summer you can often see large groups of white-clothed pilgrims hiking to or from the summit and we will show you a photo or two of them. Dewa Sanzan means "Three Mountains of Dewa" and indeed comprises the three sacred mountains of Mt. Hagurosan (羽黒山), Mt. Gassan (月山) and Mt. Yudonosan (湯殿山), clustered together in the ancient province of Dewa (modern-day Yamagata Prefecture).

We have been on Mt. Gassan three times, but we have only summited it two times. On August 10, 2005 we went to Mt. Gassan with Kazuya's parents just to see some of the lower elevation sights and flowers. Then on August 12 and 13, 2008 we summited and descended Mt. Gassan for the first time. Our third visit – and second climb and descent – was on August 6 and 7, 2011.

Both times that we stayed overnight on the mountain we stayed in the very nice summit hut. Both of those times the hut had a minimal number of guests and we could not understand how they could survive financially. Apparently Yamagata Prefecture makes up for any shortcoming of money that this hut encounters. They gave us a private room for both of our stays there. They have very nice bedding and quite adequate meals as well as beer, Japanese Saké and an assortment of snacks to go with your alcoholic drinks.

If you have no interest in flowers then there is not very much reason to challenge this mountain. The scenery is nice at the summit due to a very wide and large summit plateau, the climb is not too difficult and the crowds are not terrible, but the variety of wildflowers to be found here is just absolutely amazing. As promised above, this series of books will not concentrate on flowers however, and for that reason very few flower photos will be shown to you here.

Getting to the start of the climb is a bit difficult unless you are driving your own car. We, however, used public transit and the following photo shows the bus stop where one catches the bus to come to this mountain if one wants to approach from it's southern climbing route. Note the bus schedule, enlarged to show that only four buses per day are available to get you to the starting point. The name of this bus stop is the "Nishikawa" bus stop. It is near the Nishikawa Interchange of the Yamagata Expressway.

The second following photo shows the bus which takes you to the starting point. You'll notice that it is a mini-bus; not many people use it so there is no need for a large size bus.

When you arrive at the end of the line on this bus route there are a few inns in which you can stay overnight if you are arriving late in the day and want to wait until the following day to begin your ascent. From here, you walk up to the end of the road and then take a simple chair lift up to the point where most people begin their ascent. We'll show you a map quite soon so that you can get a better idea of the lay of the land, so to speak.

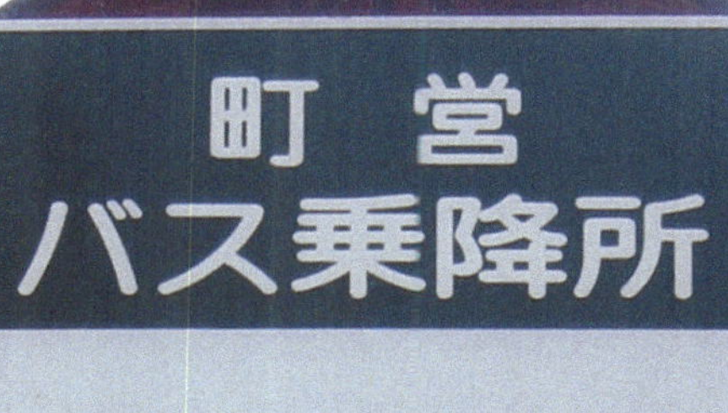

西　川　Ｉ　Ｃ

H20.4.1	道路混雑等のため遅れる場合がありますのでご了承ください。	
行先	姥沢	
経由 時	間沢 月山銘水館 志津	
7		
8		
9	10	
10		
11	20	
12		
13		
14	15	
15		
16	25	

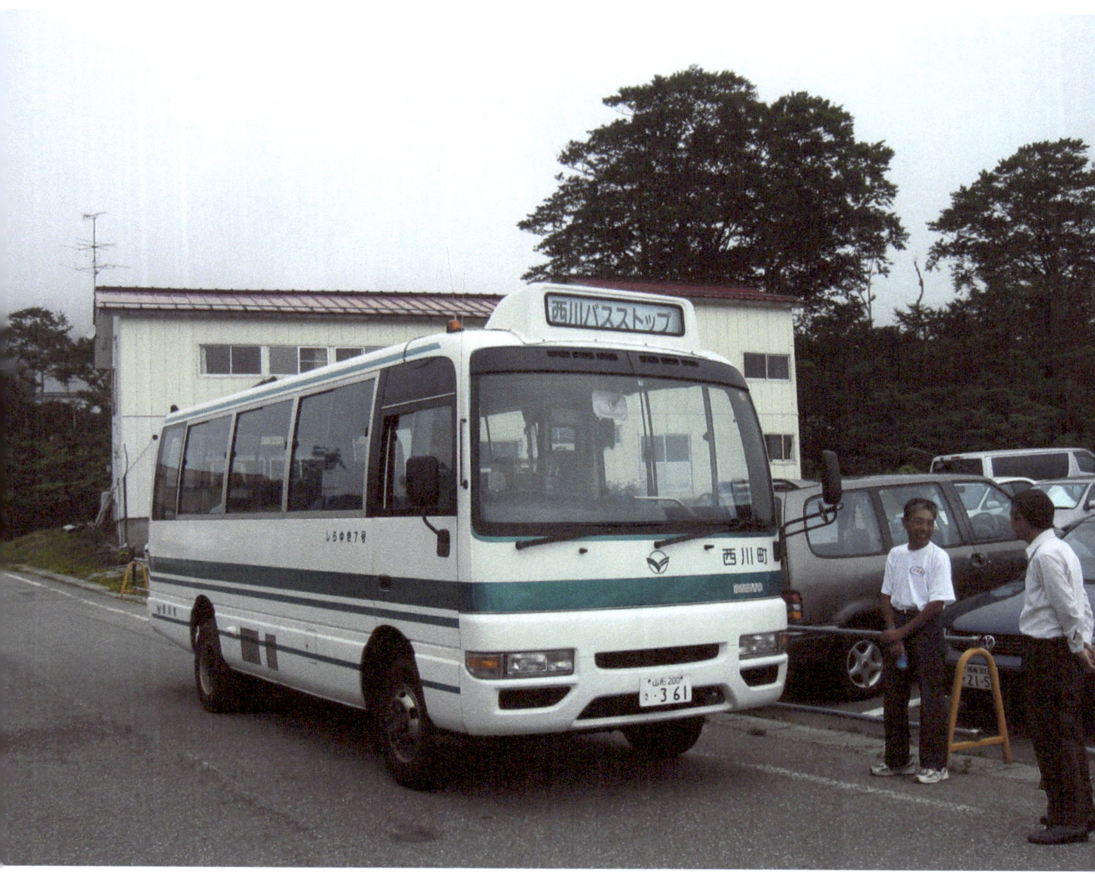

On the following page is the map which we promised. On this map, the 1. annotation indicates the bus stop shown on this page. The Japanese writing there indicates that it is a forty-five minute bus ride to the Nishikawa bus stop and also says that there is space for 500 cars in the parking lot here. We must wonder if the parking lot ever becomes full. The 2. annotation on the map shows the chair lift.

On the page following the map, the upper photo shows the top of the chair lift and the person standing there taking photographs is me. This photo was taken in 2011 and the weather was wonderful.

The lower photo on the page after the map shows a view of the top of the chair lift from approximately 100 meters up the trail or somewhere thereabouts. This photo was taken in 2008 and, as you can see, the clouds are rolling around us as we hike. Note how nice and wide the trail is at this point. It is also "rocked" as you can see in the photo.

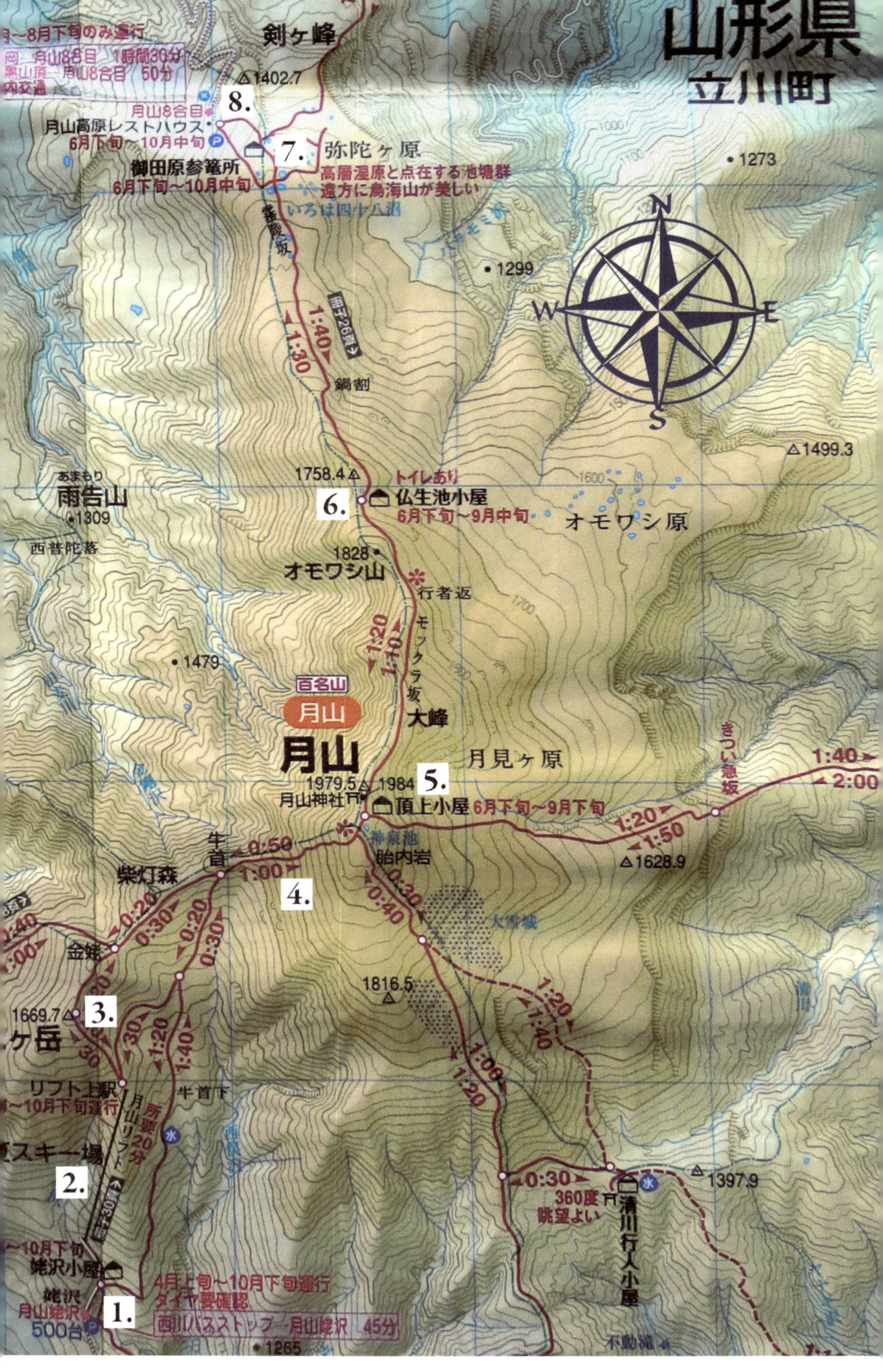
山形県
立川町
剣ヶ峰
△1402.7
8.
月山高原レストハウス・
6月下旬〜10月中旬
御田原参籠所
6月下旬〜10月中旬
7.
弥陀ヶ原
高層湿原と点在する池塘群
遠方に鳥海山が美しい
いろは四十八沼
・1273
・1299
N
W E
S
1:40
1:30
串子26貫
鍋割
1758.4△
トイレあり
6.
仏生池小屋
6月下旬〜9月中旬
オモワシ原
△1499.3
雨告山
・1309
西普陀落
1828・
オモワシ山
行者返
1:20
1:10
モックラ坂
大峰
・1479
百名山
月山
月山
1979.5△ 1984
月山神社
月見ヶ原
5.
頂上小屋 6月下旬〜9月下旬
1:40
2:00
きつい急坂
牛首 0:50
柴灯森
1:00
神泉池
胎内岩
1:20
1:50
△1628.9
4.
0:30
0:40
0:20
0:30
0:20
0:30
大雪城
金姥
1:20
1:40
1816.5
△
1:20
1:40
1669.7△
3.
ヶ岳
0:30
0:30
1:20
1:40
牛首下
リフト上駅
〜10月下旬運行
月山リフト
所要20分
水
1:00
1:20
スキー場
2.
0:30
360度
眺望よい
清川行人小屋
水
△1397.9
姥沢小屋
姥沢
月山姥沢
500台
1.
4月上旬〜10月下旬運行
ダイヤ要確認
西川バスストップ 月山姥沢 45分
・1265
不動滝

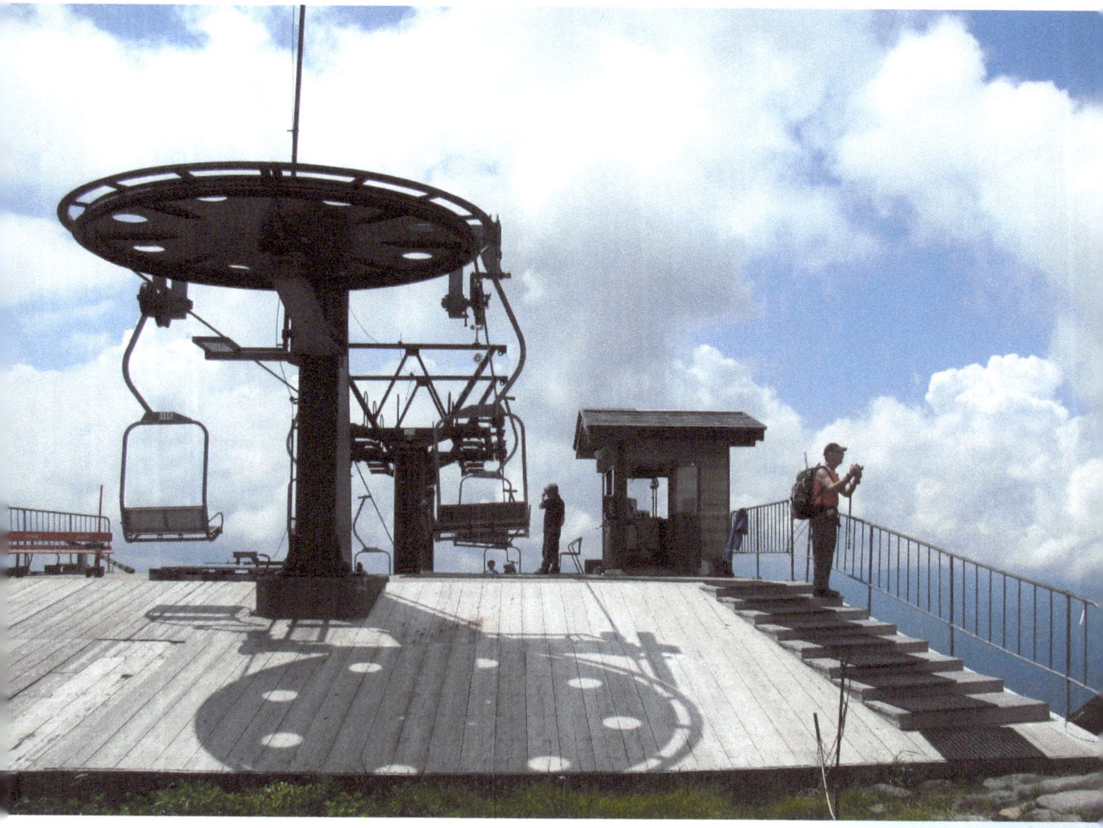

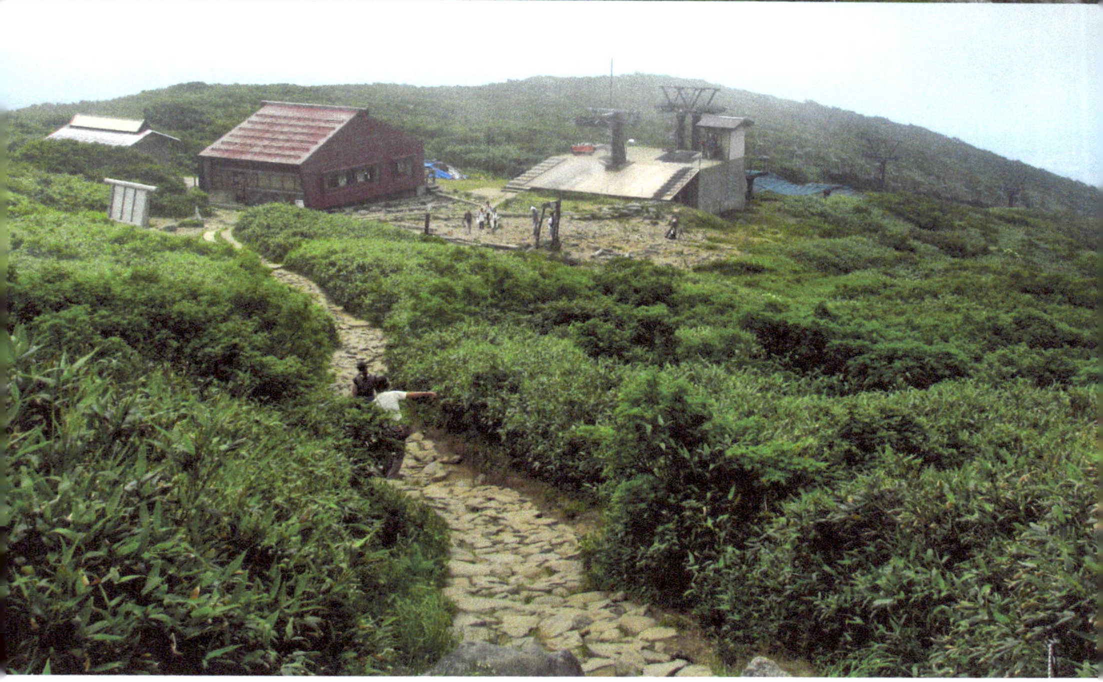

Okay, let's continue. Now we are headed up the trail which goes to the left at the top of the chair lift and we are going to be at Ubagatake (annotation 3. on the map) in a short time. For us it was about a forty minute climb from the top of the chair lift to Ubagatake, but we stop very often and spend five or ten minutes taking photos of flowers and scenery, so if you're not as enthusiastic about photos as we are, then you can expect to do this part of the climb more quickly. There is a lot of very nice scenery on this route to Ubagatake and the flowers are amazing.

Below is one shot which shows a very large snowfield. This was about half of the distance from the top of the chair lift to the summit of Ubagatake. Note some people in the upper left corner.

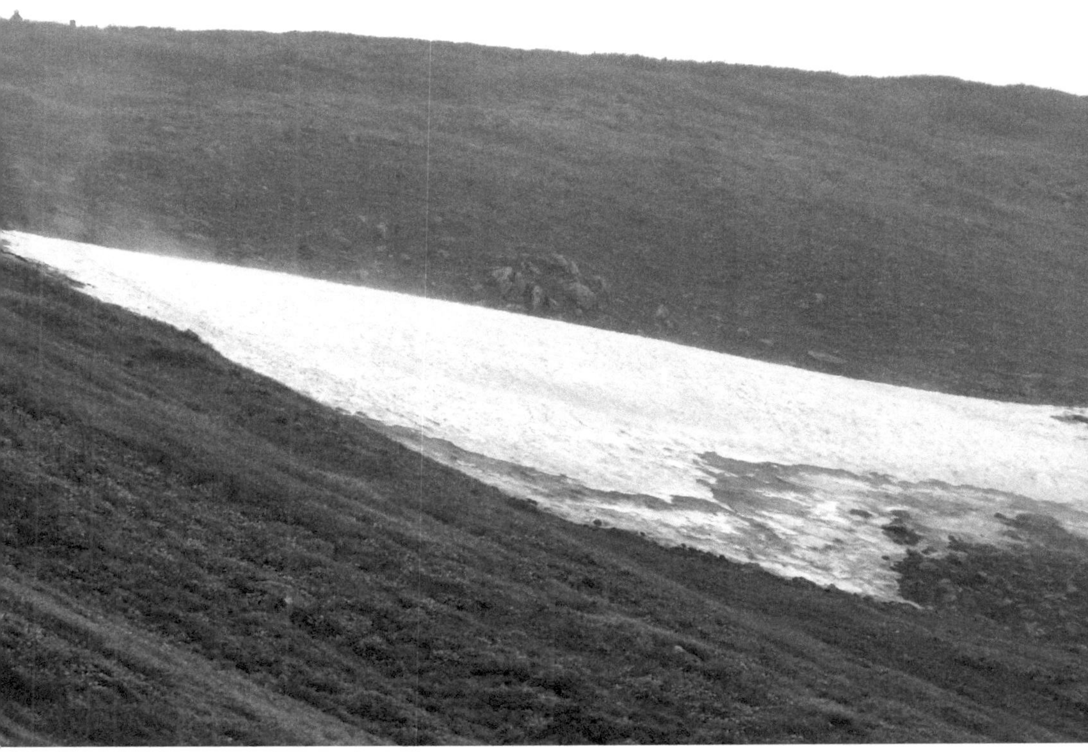

On the following page is another photo taken between the top of the chair lift and Ubagatake. It shows a small pond which is quite literally surrounded by flowers. Our style is to stop and take several photos like this, as well as several macro-photos of the flowers themselves.

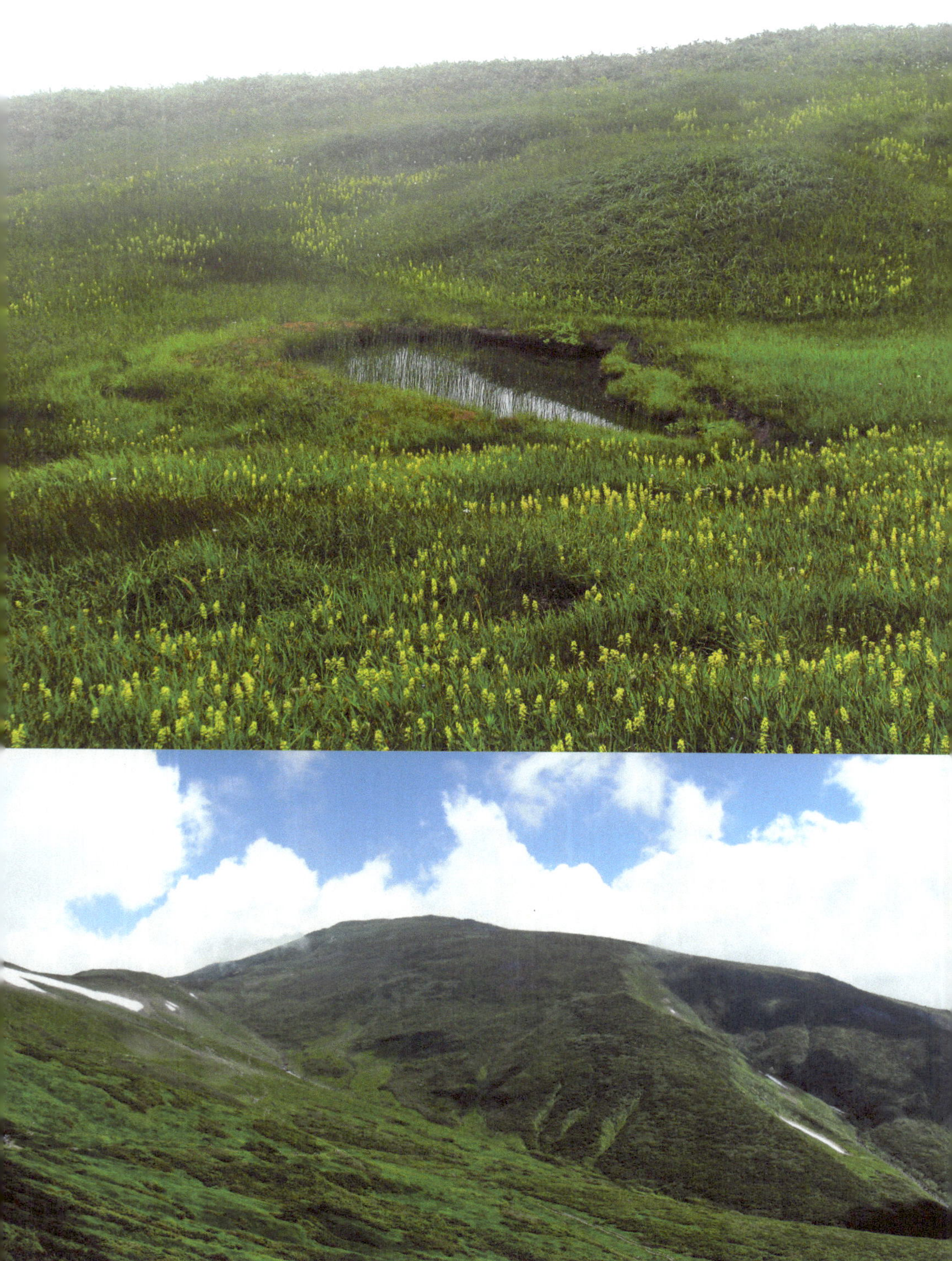

The lower photo on the facing page is another scenery shot which we were able to capture as we got closer to Ubagatake. Such amazing green colors, who knew that greens like this could exist?

The following photo is basically the same as the lower one on the facing page, but it is shifted more to the left. Again, note the brilliant greens and also note the snowfield that we will eventually climb past. You can also see several climbers in this photo if you study it a bit.

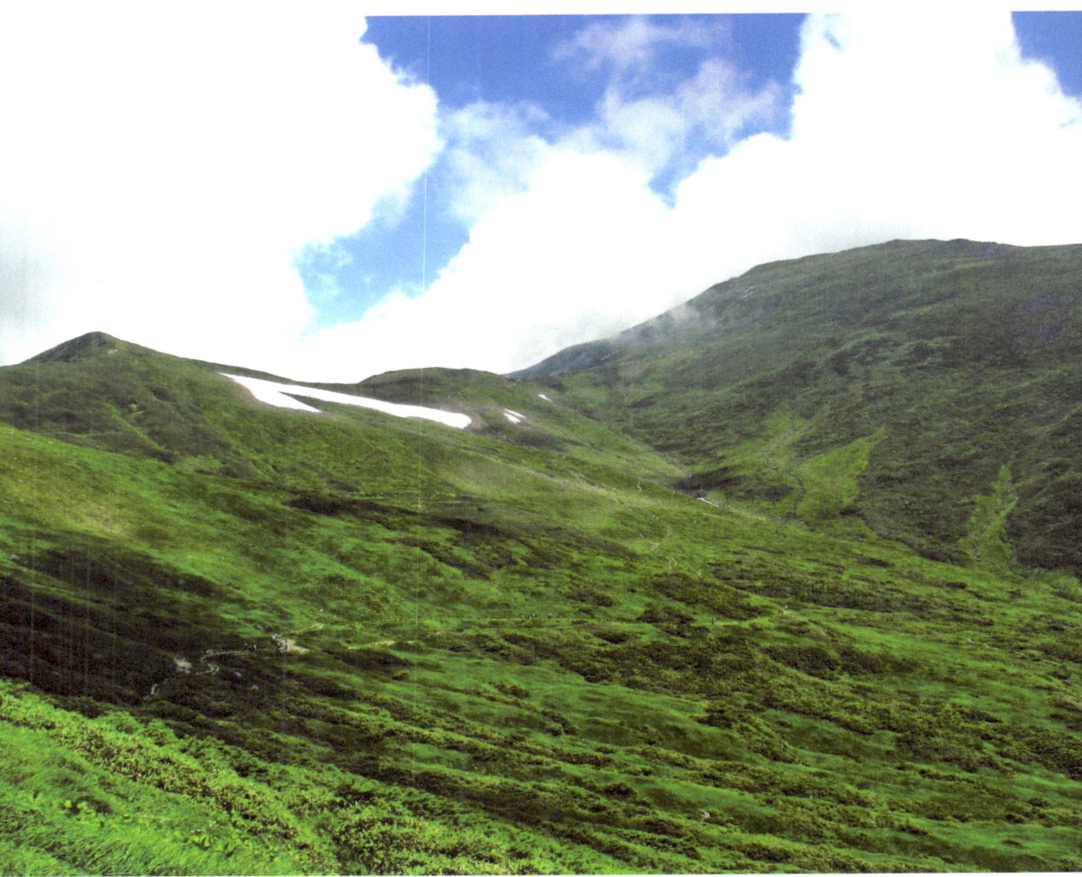

The following image shows two separate photos of each of us at Ubagatake, which is the 1669.7 m peak just to the left of the 3. annotation on the map back on page 13. Note how happy we look, it's because we are having a great time. These two photos were taken in 2008 when we summited this mountain for the first time.

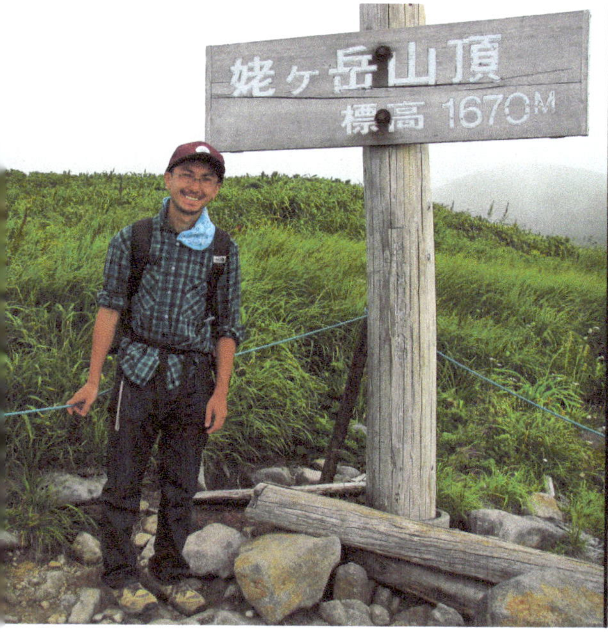

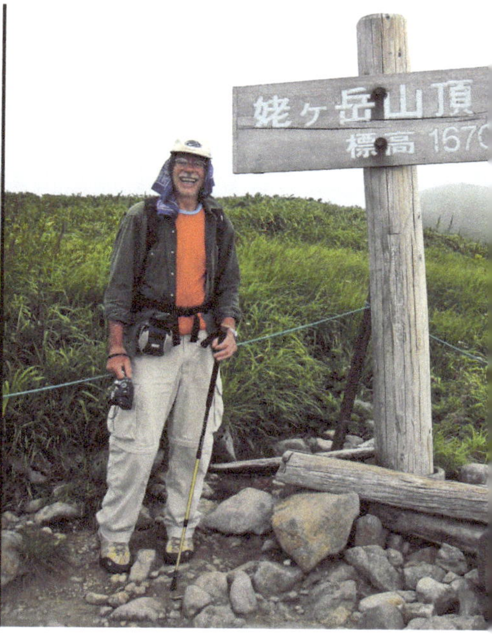

Below – a view from Ubagatake with some beautiful green colors.

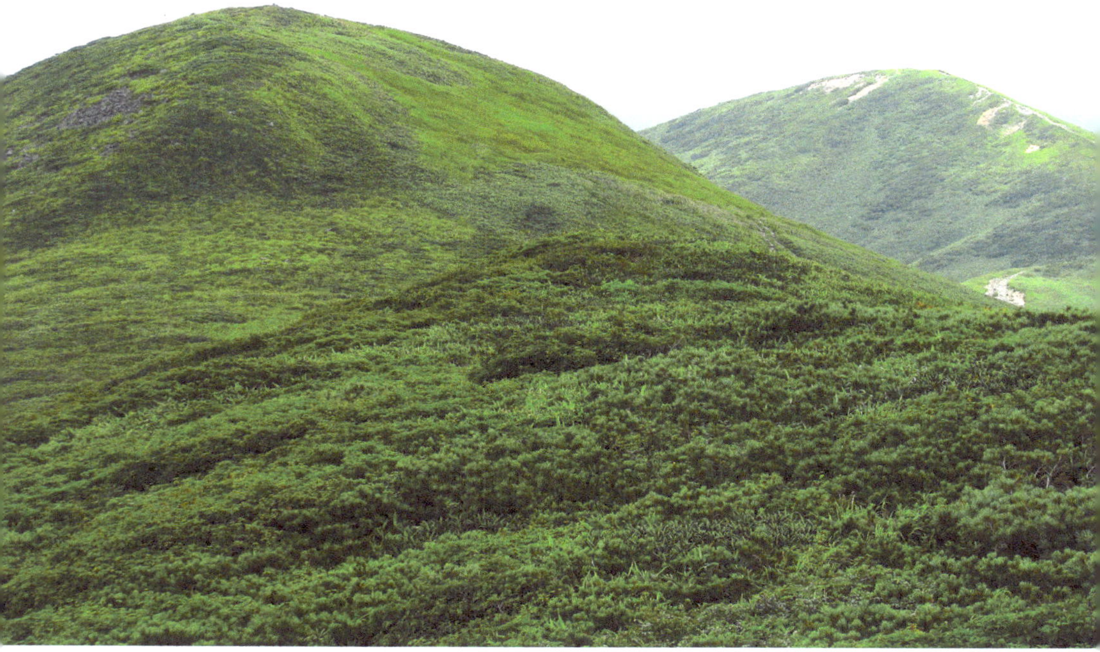

Ubagatake is the first place where either one of us ever saw Edelweiss in bloom. That was on our 2008 climb and we have seen it in several places since then. The species which we saw was *Leontopodium fauriei*. We just have to show you one photo of it (below). In this photo the flowers are well past their peak of beauty, but one of the things about Edelweiss is that the flowers hang on for a long time.

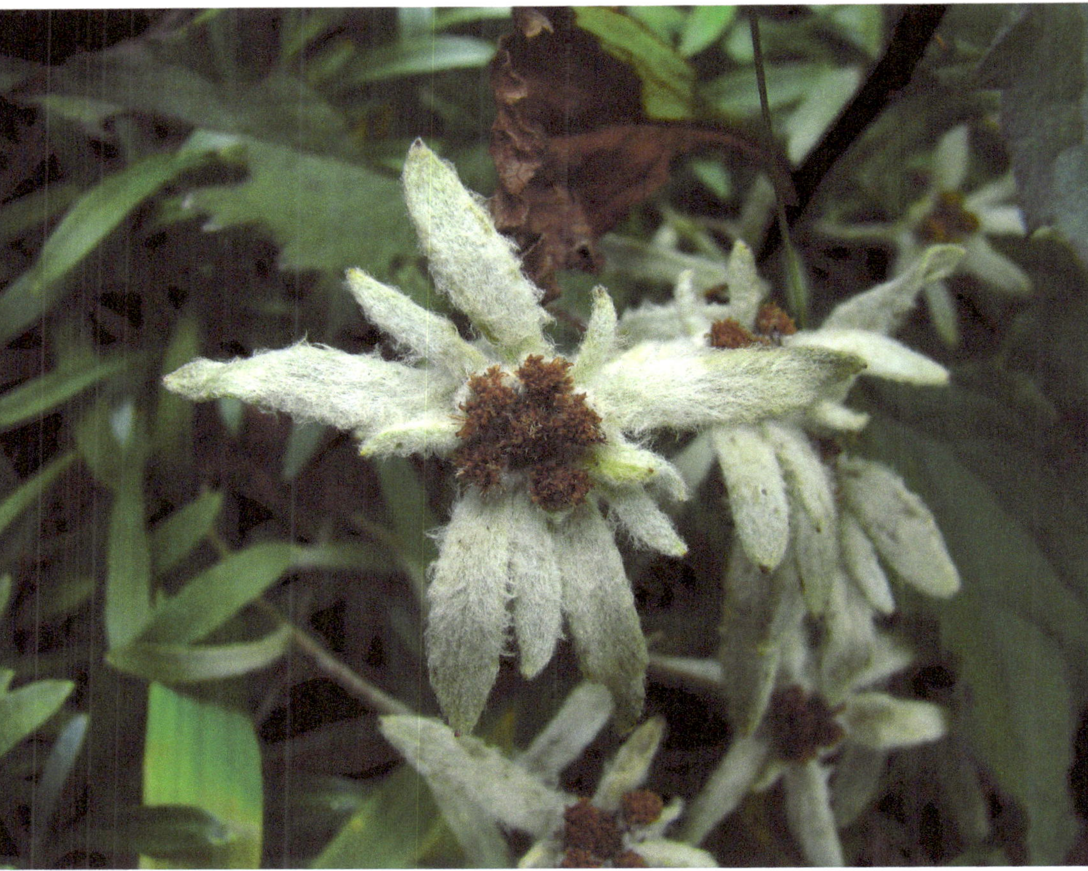

Below is a photo of this same species of Edelweiss which was taken at a different place and at a different time of the year – when the flowers were at their peak. It is included here merely to show you what a flower at its peak looks like.

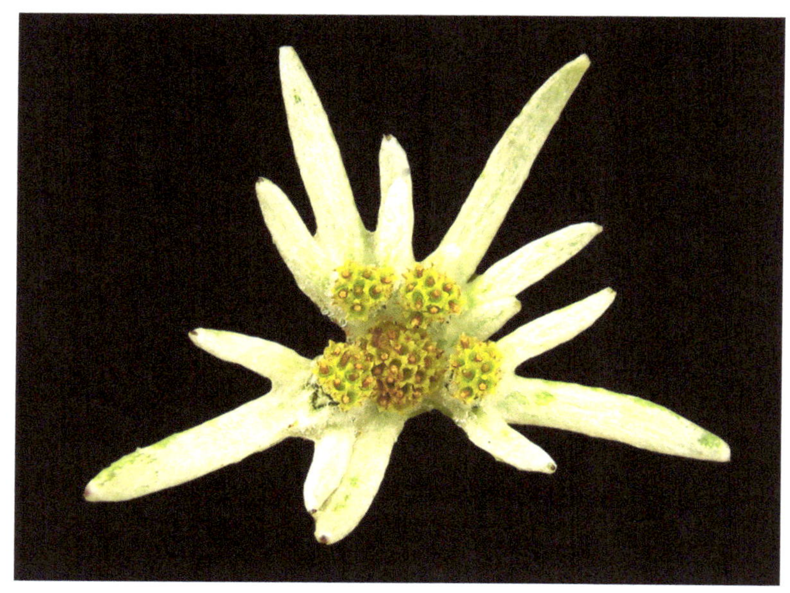

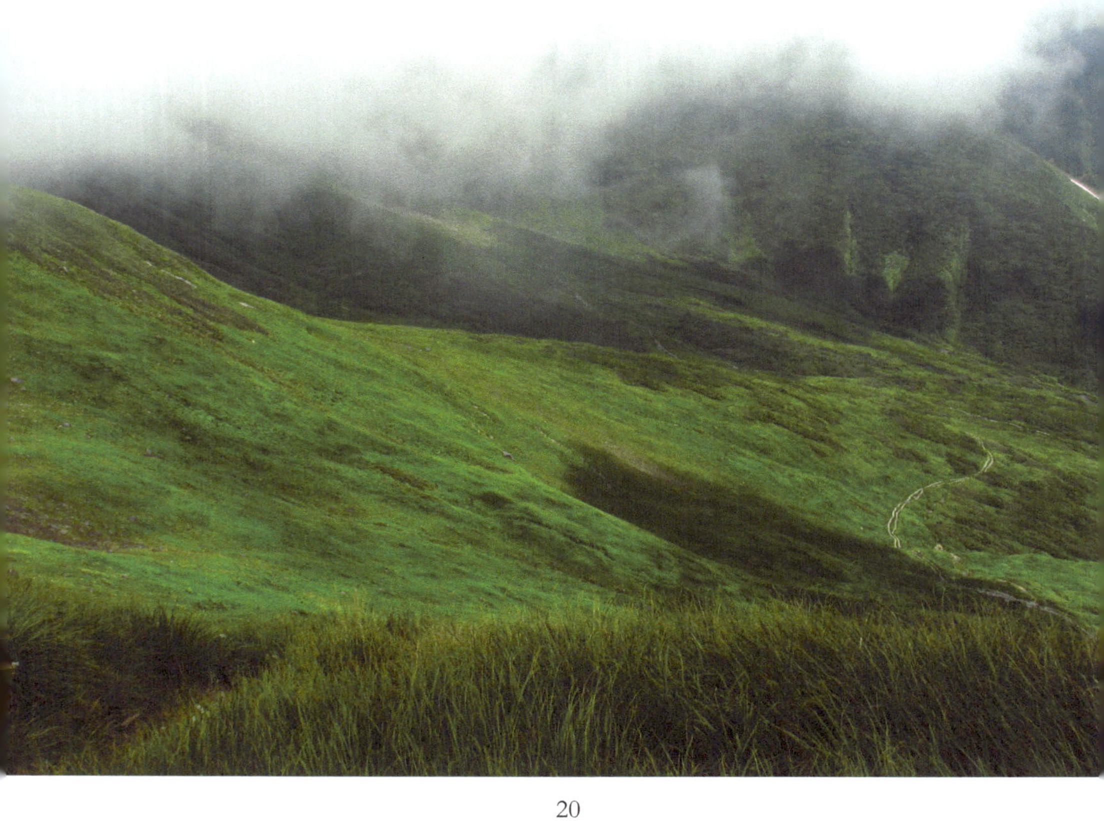

The previous photo, taken during our 2011 climb, was shot just after we had left Ubagatake and were headed towards the 4. annotation on the map (page 13). You'll probably notice the trail down below us – if you look at the map you can see the lower trail to the right.

Now we're going to show you more incredible green scenery. You can see on the map, that between Ubagatake and the next junction to the north (Ushikubi) (牛首), the junction closest to the 4. annotation, the trail follows along a ridge. As we follow along that ridge we'll see some very nice scenery, a large snowfield and then after a while we'll arrive at the very long slope which marks the 4. annotation.

In the photo below you'll surely notice that a portion of it has been outlined. That outlined area indicates the approximate area which you can see in the photo on the following page. Both of these photos were taken during our 2008 climb. On the left side of the photo immediately below you will notice some snowfields.

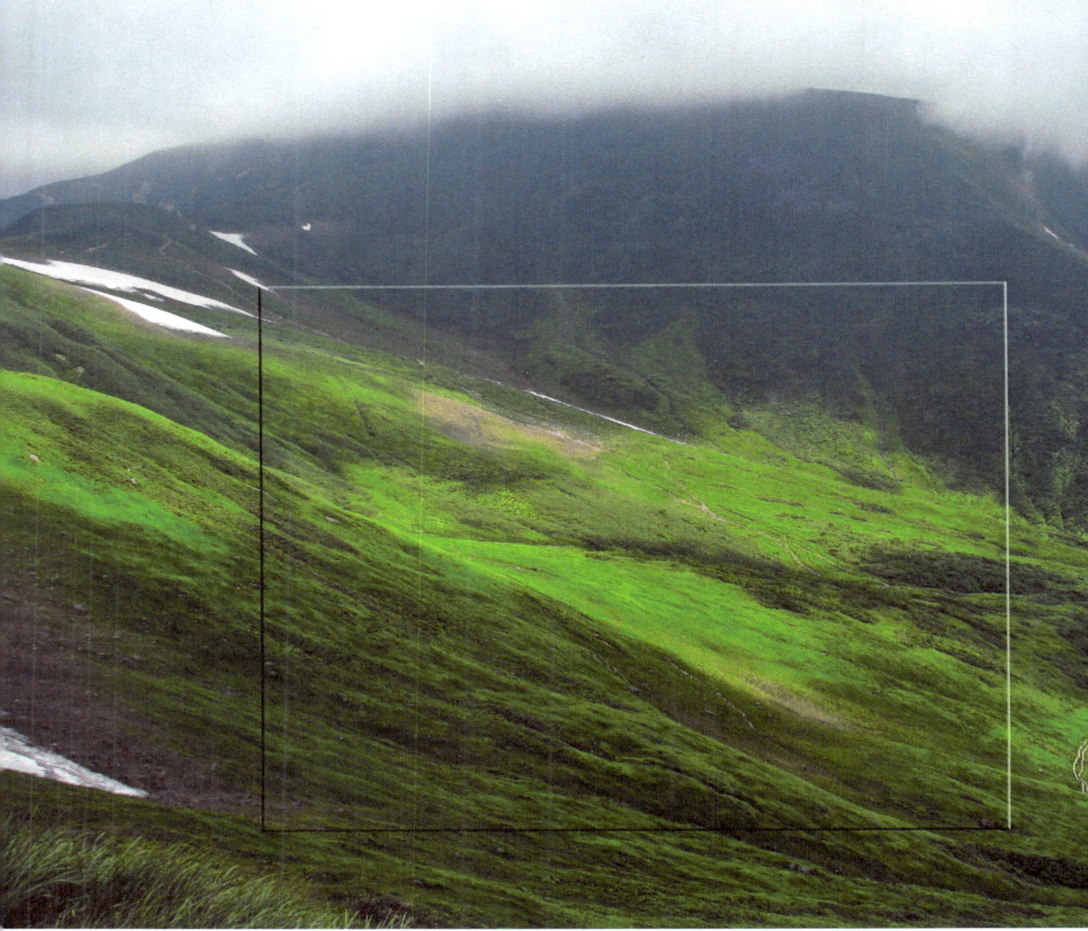

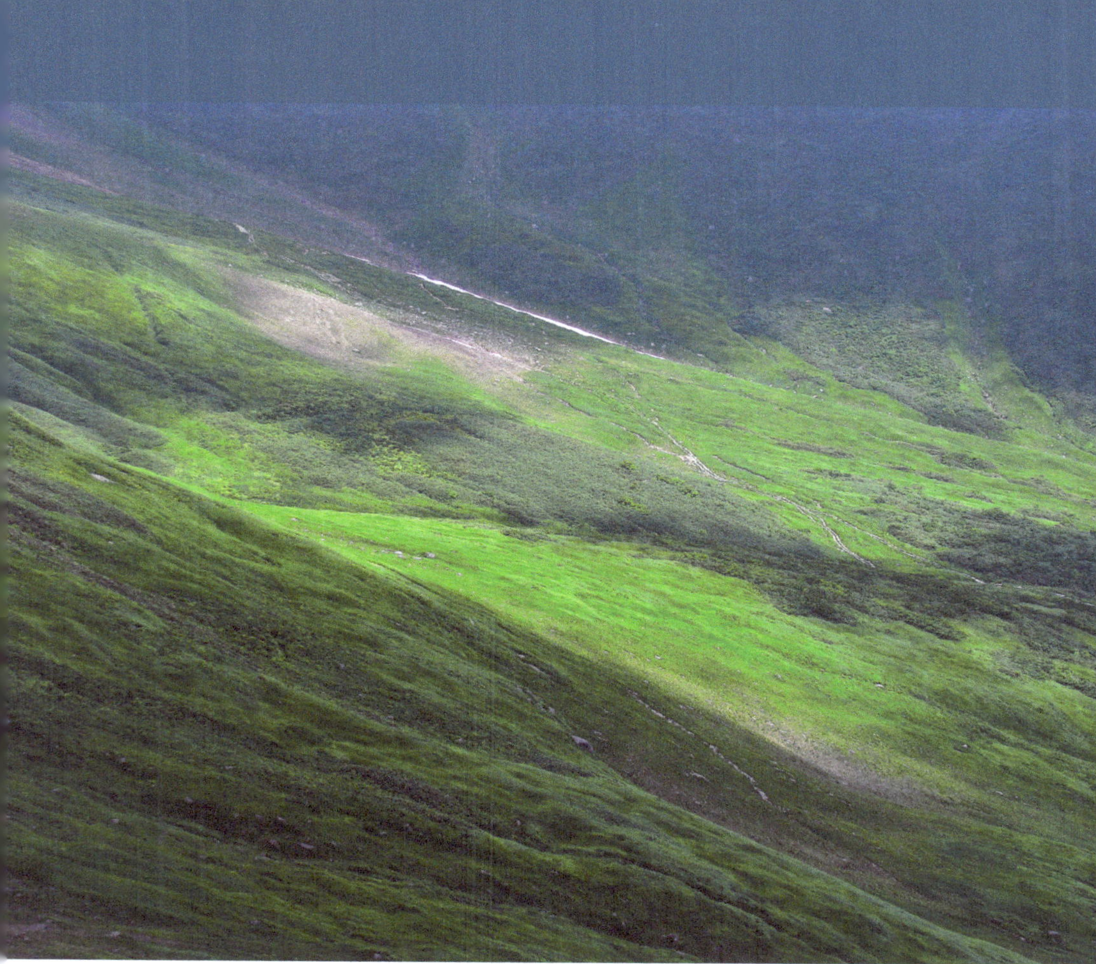

Okay, this photo immediately above is zoomed in to that outlined area of the photo on page 21. Note how it is sunny near the center of the photo, but that the clouds are creating shadows over most of the remainder of the photo. On both of our climbs of this mountain the weather was similar to this – clouds coming and going, threatening to rain on us and then disappearing and getting sunny again. It was weird weather, but very fortunately we did not get rained on. Also, very fortunately, the clouds did keep disappearing so that we could have some nice views and get plenty of photos.

Now we'll show you a few more photos which were taken along the trail between Ubagatake and Ushikubi (牛首).

The upper facing page photo shows me with a big smile as we hike along this excellent trail, notice that I am shaded – there is a cloud rolling by at the moment.

The lower photo on the facing page shows a steaming snowfield – interesting, wouldn't you agree.

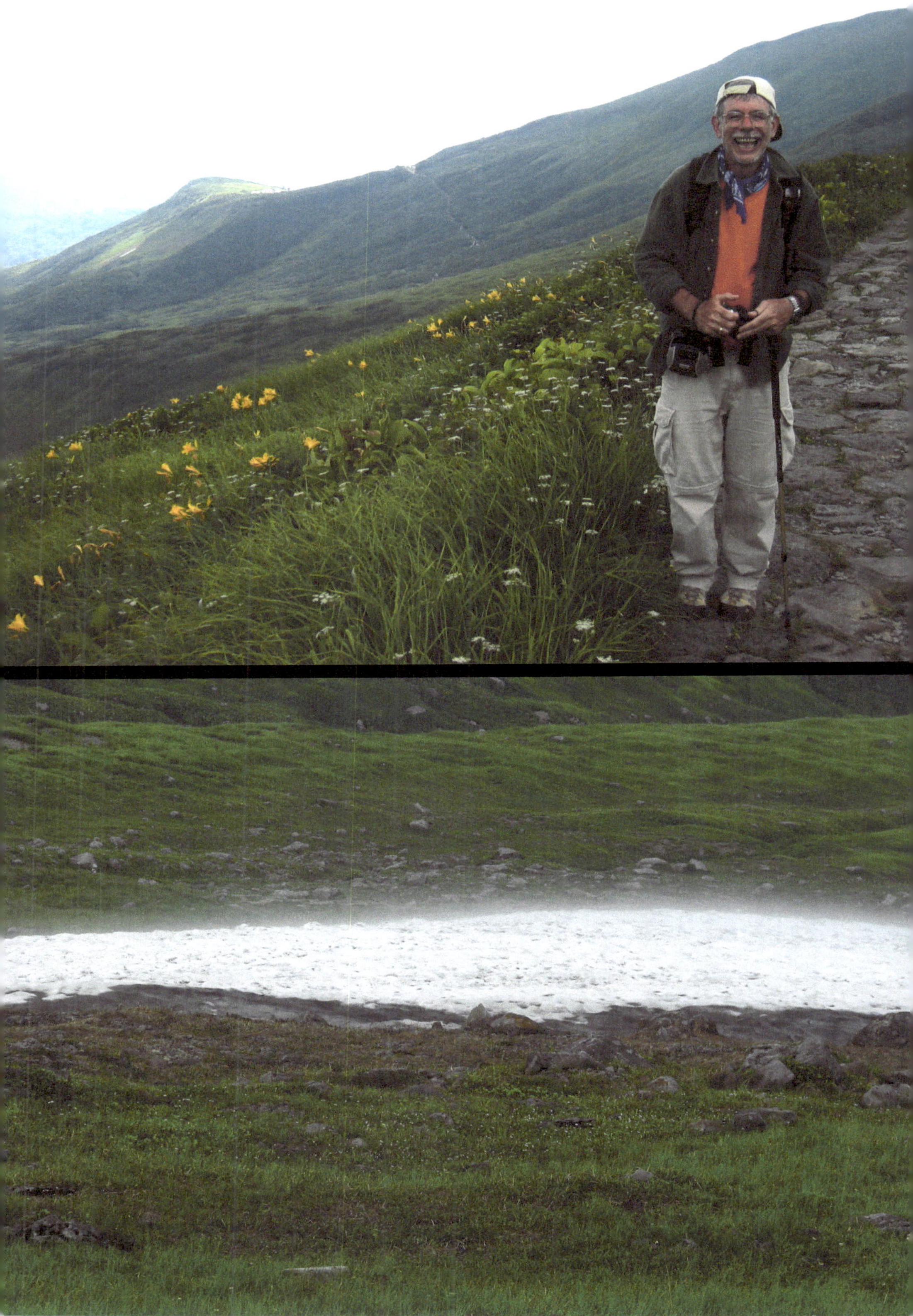

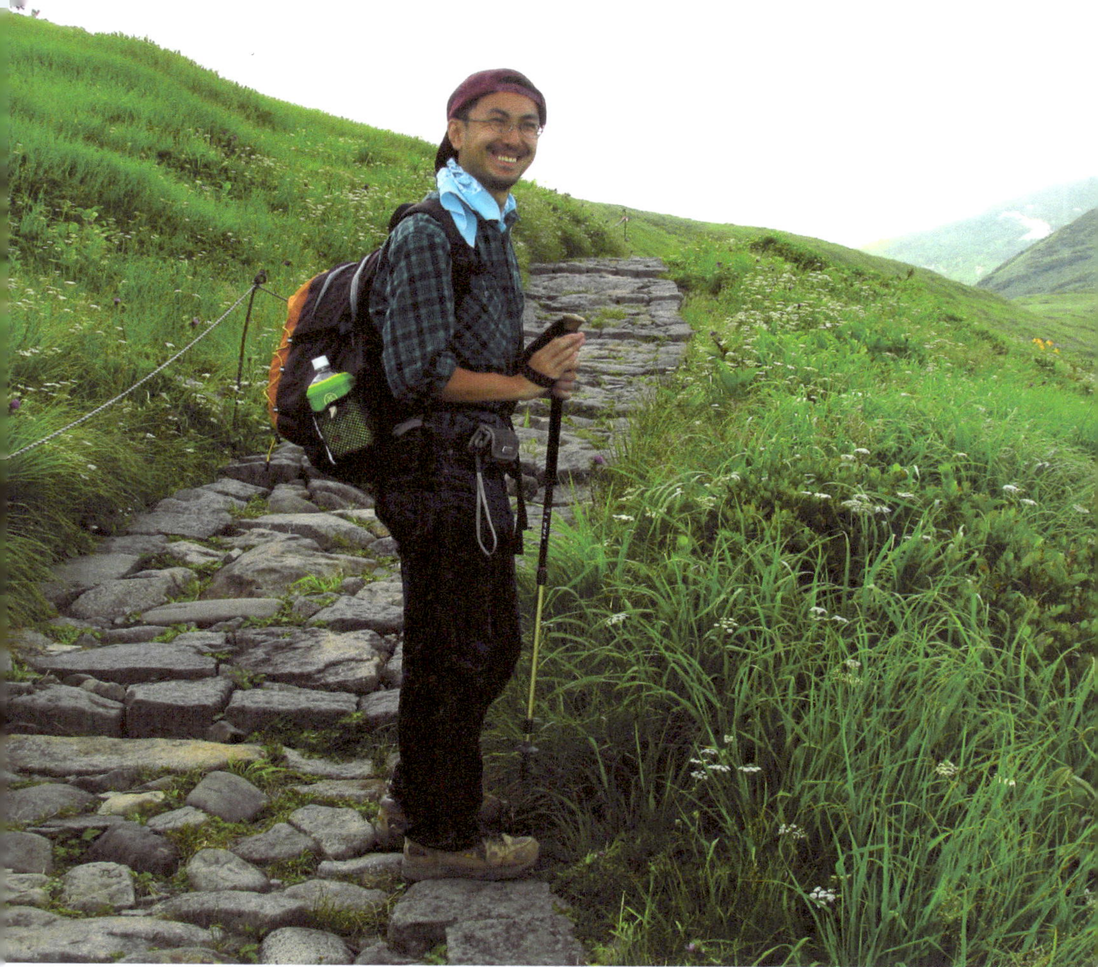

The photo immediately above shows Kazuya wearing a big smile and in this photo you can get a better feel for what this trail is like. It is not smooth, you have to more or less constantly keep watching your feet or else one of those rock edges is going to catch you and knock you down. In both of these photos which we took of each other, you may note all of the flowers – we are both pretty much surrounded by flowers on all sides. Remember, we previously said that if you have no interest in flowers then there is not very much reason to challenge this mountain. You can see that the trail is not steep, nor is it challenging. You can find five and six year old children hiking on this mountain – although it seemed that at some point the parents had to give in and help them along. It's a long hike, even if not that difficult.

The next photo shows the boardwalk which serves as the trail through this semi-wet area and also shows the beautiful green colors here. The boardwalk begins after the rocky trail ends, between Ubagatake and Ushikubi. This is a 2008 photo. You can again see several snowfields in this photo.

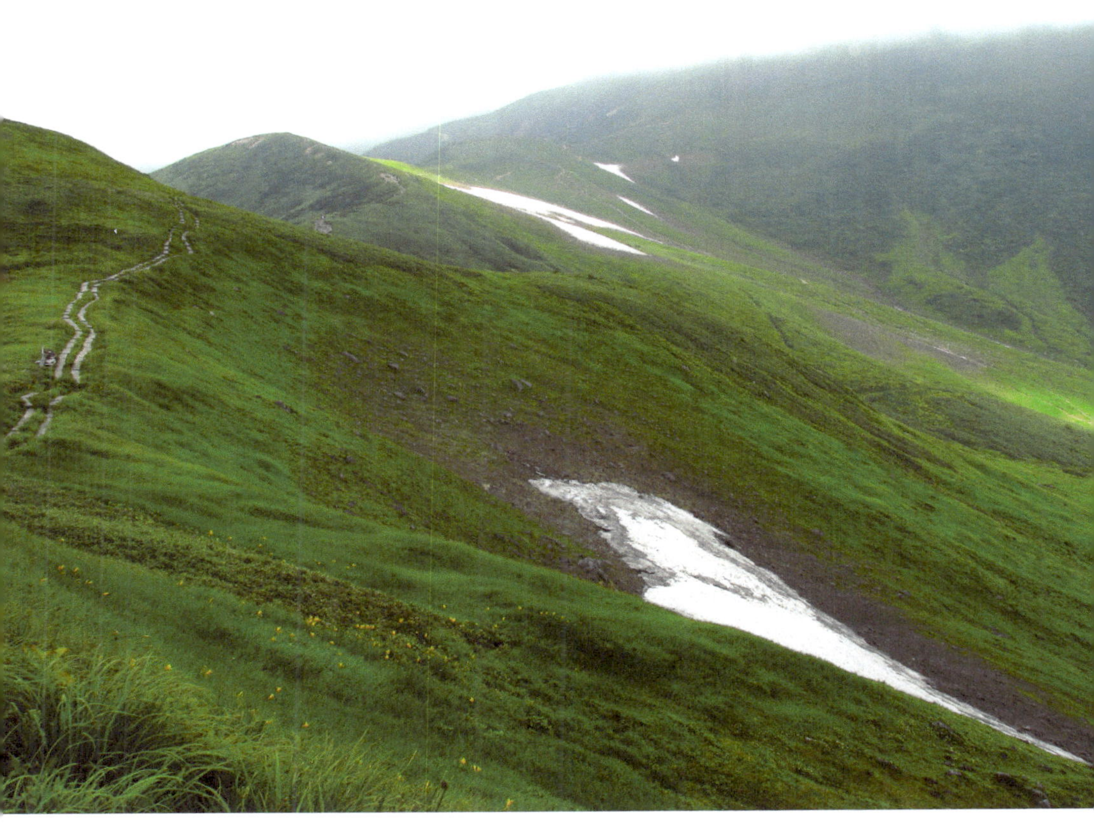

The next two photos also show that portion of the trail which is boardwalk. The lady is apparently asking the gentleman which way the trail goes, as you can see him pointing the direction to her. What you should especially note here is the clouds. This photo was taken at 12:12 PM on August 6, 2011.

The lower photo on the following page, with no people showing (where did they go?) was taken at 12:15 PM on the same date. One of the reasons we are showing you these two photos is so that you can appreciate just how quickly the conditions can change on the mountain. Surely you have read that it can happen like this, but have you ever experienced it? This is why a person has to always come prepared for any and every possible type of weather.

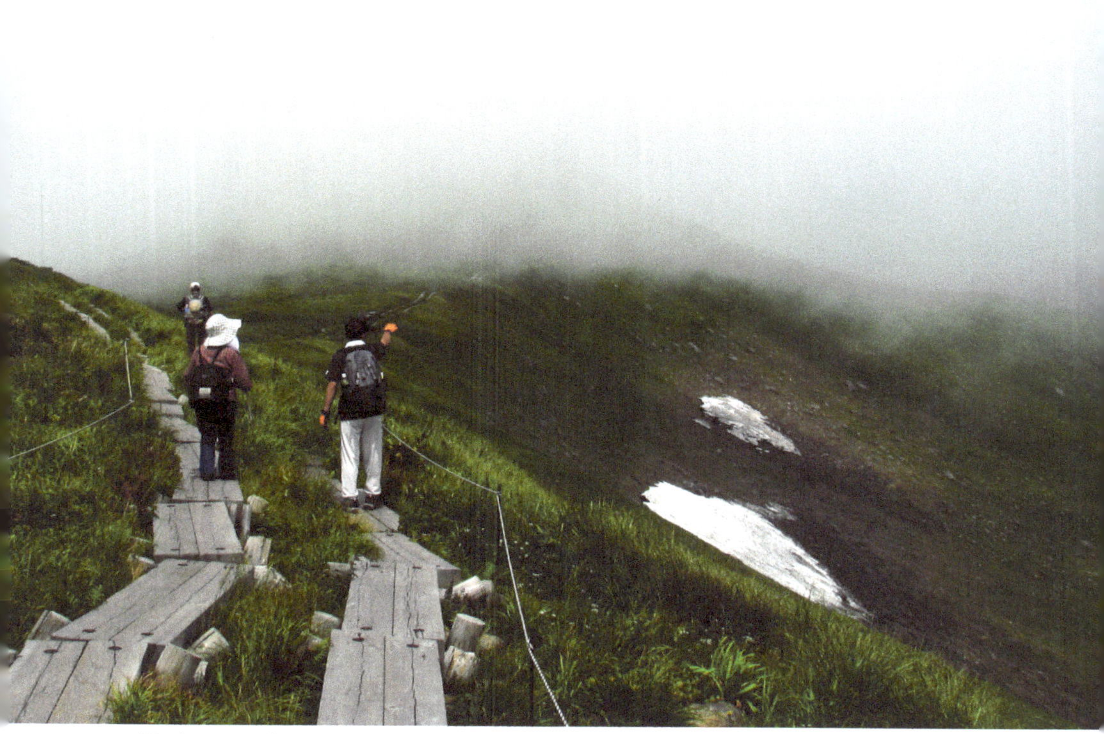

Below – the peak ahead and just about at the center is Ushikubi.

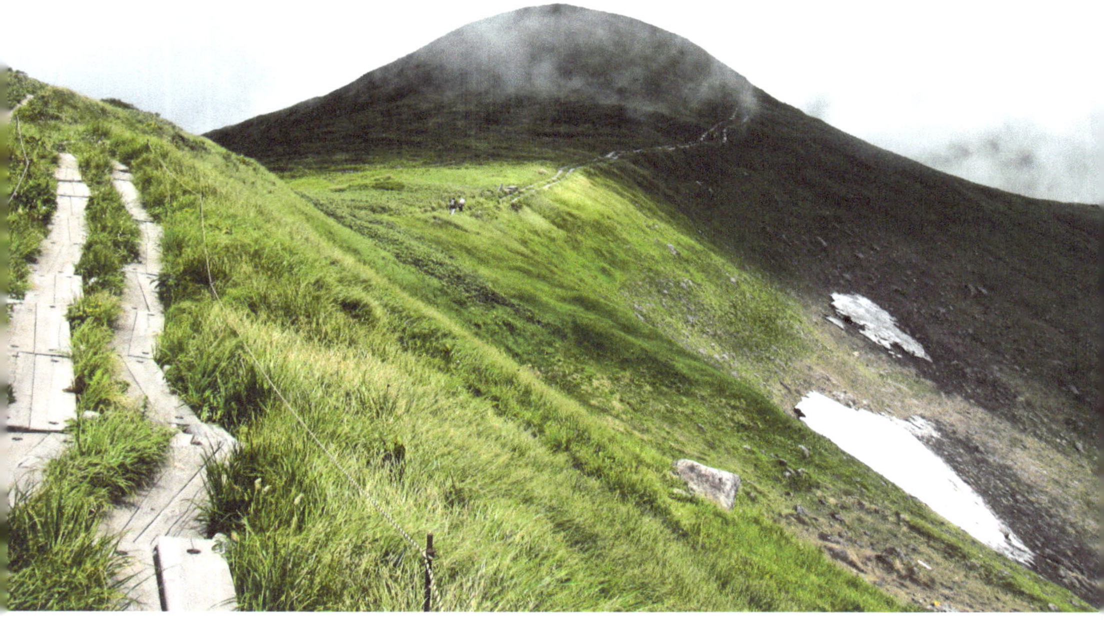

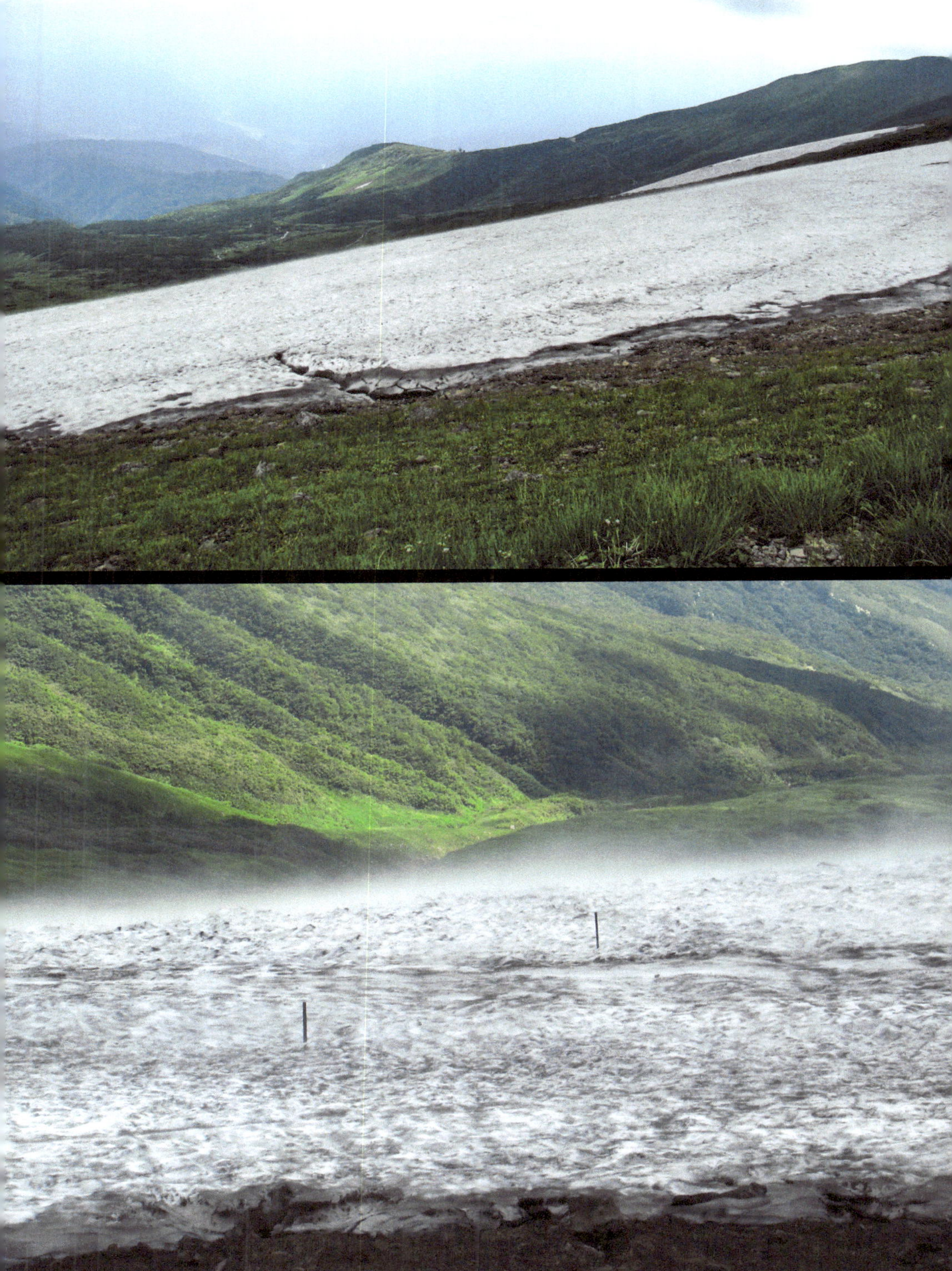

On the previous page we showed you two photos of a snowfield which was very prevalent in both 2008 and also 2011. In fact, in 2011 there was a person skiing on it. The snowfield is not excessively large, so the skier was able to ski for only about two minutes and then had to walk back up to the top of it and do it again. It did not look like very much fun to us, but who are we to judge? If you study the upper photo (a 2008 photo) very closely you can even find the top of the chair lift. In the lower photo (a 2011 photo) you'll notice some wooden stakes stuck in the snow. It appeared that they were placed by that skier to mark the safe zone to ski within.

This following photo was taken in 2011, most likely just as we were rounding the summit area of Ushikubi. Note how beautiful the weather is right now. You'll also note that we are back on a rock trail. The peak ahead – in the distance – is the summit area of Mt. Gassan.

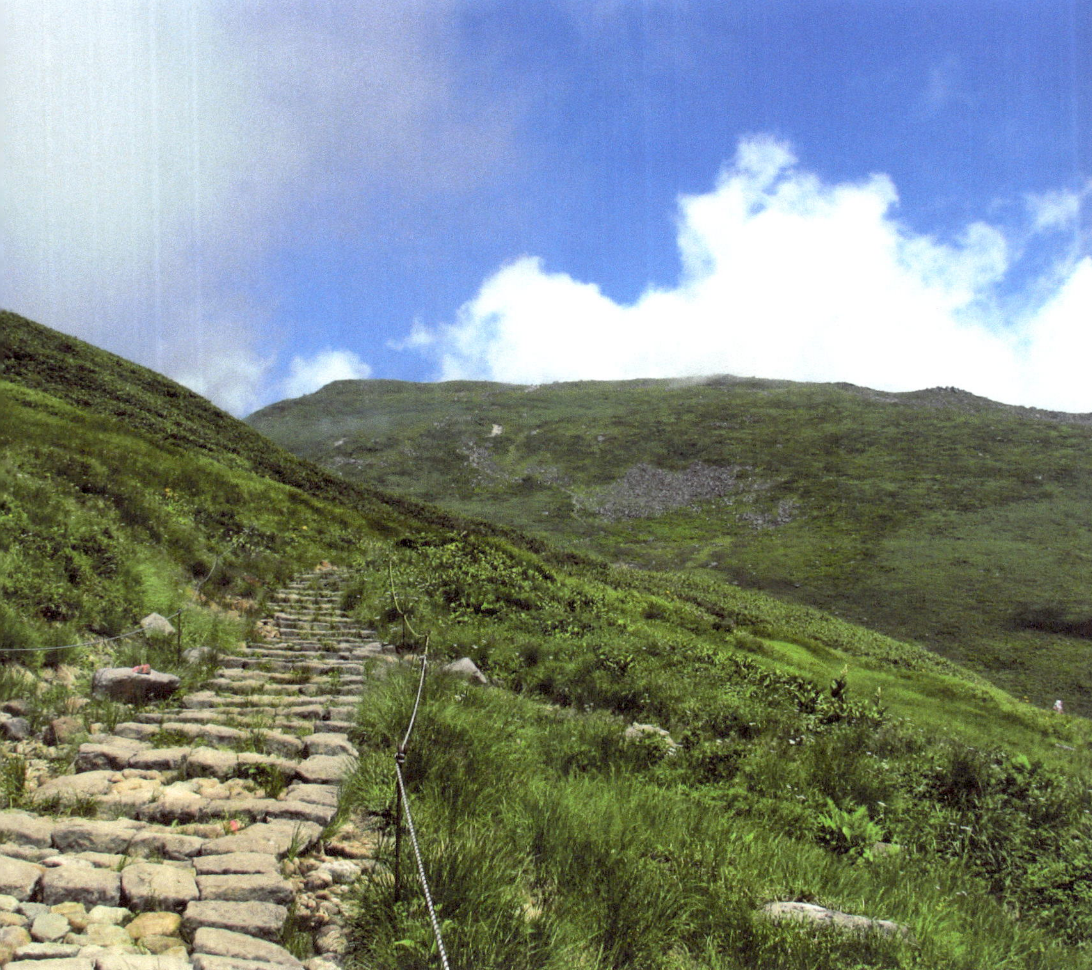

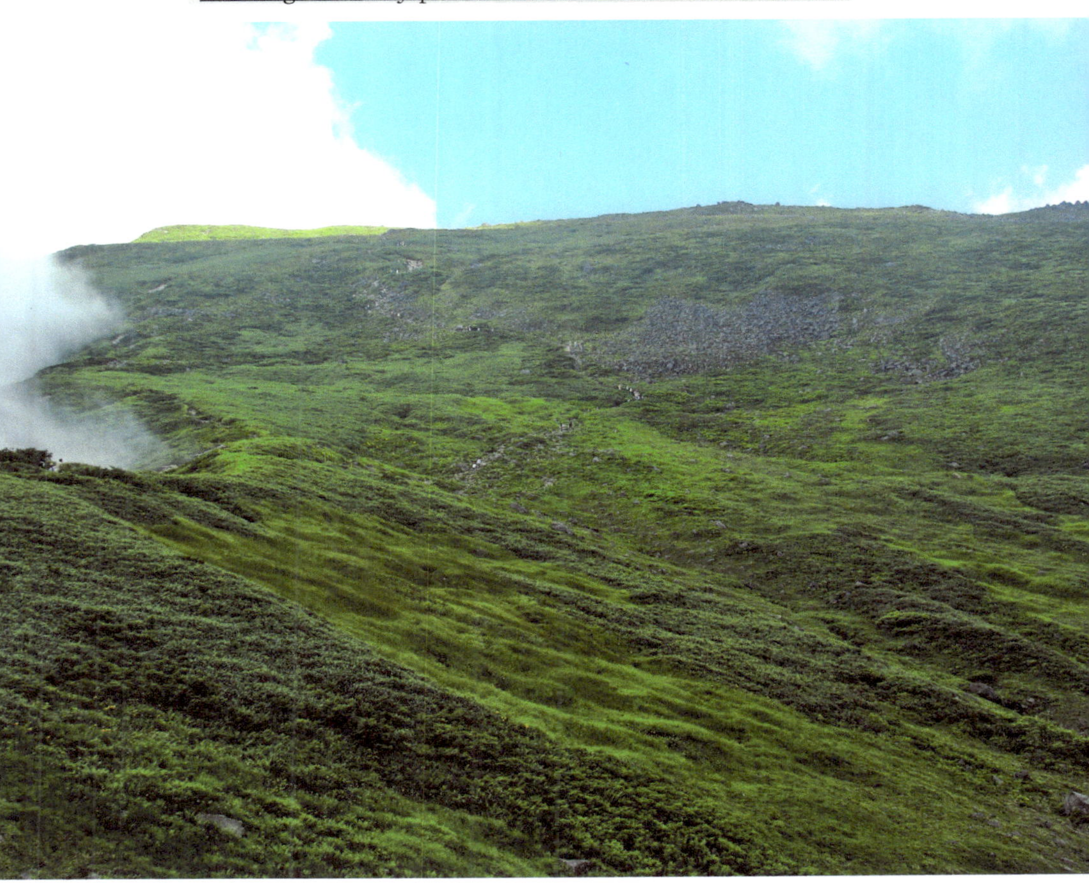

The photo above was taken just after we rounded the peak of Ushi-kubi, and the area ahead is what is designated with the 4. annotation on the map. You'll note on the map that immediately after Ushikubi the area to the north drops off very steeply. This photo shows that the clouds are coming up against that steep slope on the left and are probably getting ready to come rolling to this side of that steep slope.

The next photo (on the following page) shows the long slope which is shown by the 4. annotation on the map back on page 13. This photo was taken near the bottom of that slope and you can see several people in this photo trudging up this final slope before they reach the summit. The photo does not give a good indication of how steep this slope actually is; it is steeper than it appears, although not excessively steep. This is where many of the younger hikers get too tired to continue and have to be either carried or at least helped by their parents. It looked very difficult for people who were carrying young children.

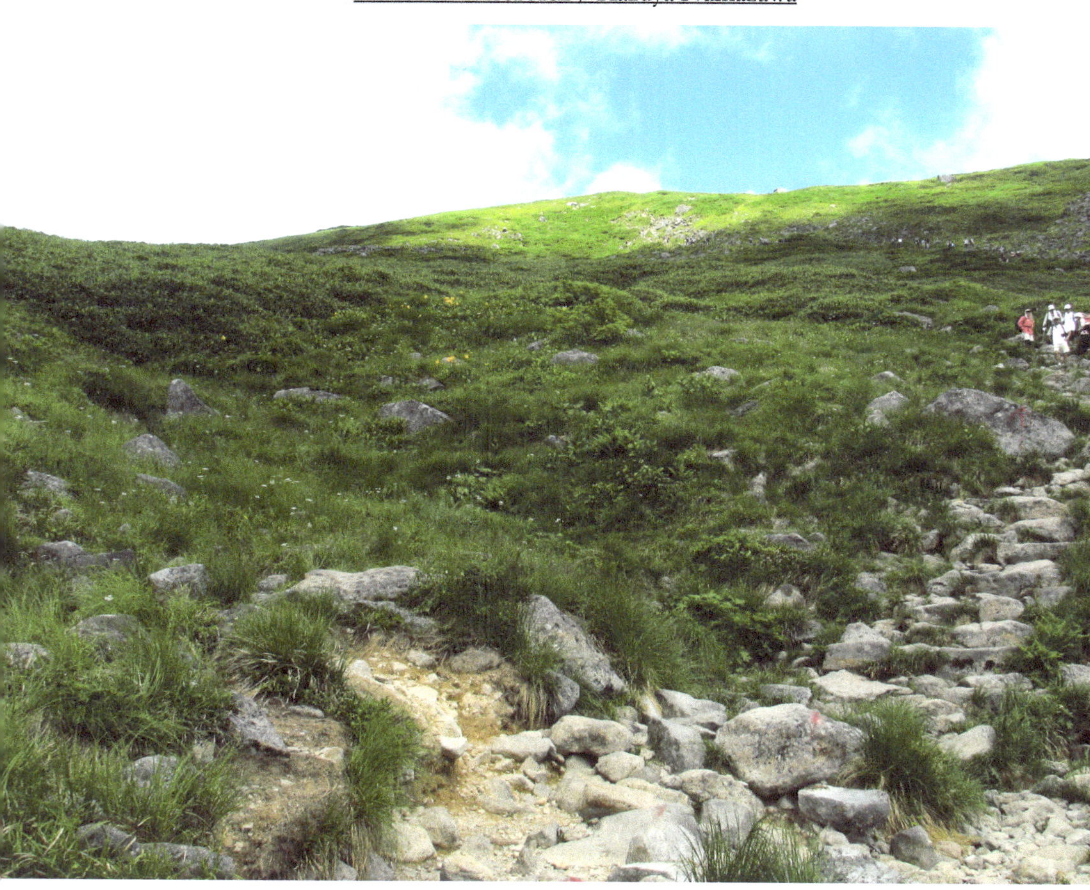

The following two photos, shown on the facing page, were taken when we were probably about one-half of the distance up that slope referred to above, which is marked by the 4. annotation on the map. The first photo was taken on August 12, 2008 at 2:07 PM and the lower photo was taken on August 6, 2011 at 1:43 PM. Two interesting things which you should note in these two photos is, #1, the difference in the weather – in 2008 it was quite a bit hazier than it was in 2011, and #2 the difference in the size of the snowfields down below us. In 2008 the snowfields were noticeably larger than in 2011. In the lower photo you can also see some people taking a break alongside the trail; remember, just above we told you that this trail is steeper than it appears in these photos. Please try to keep that in mind.

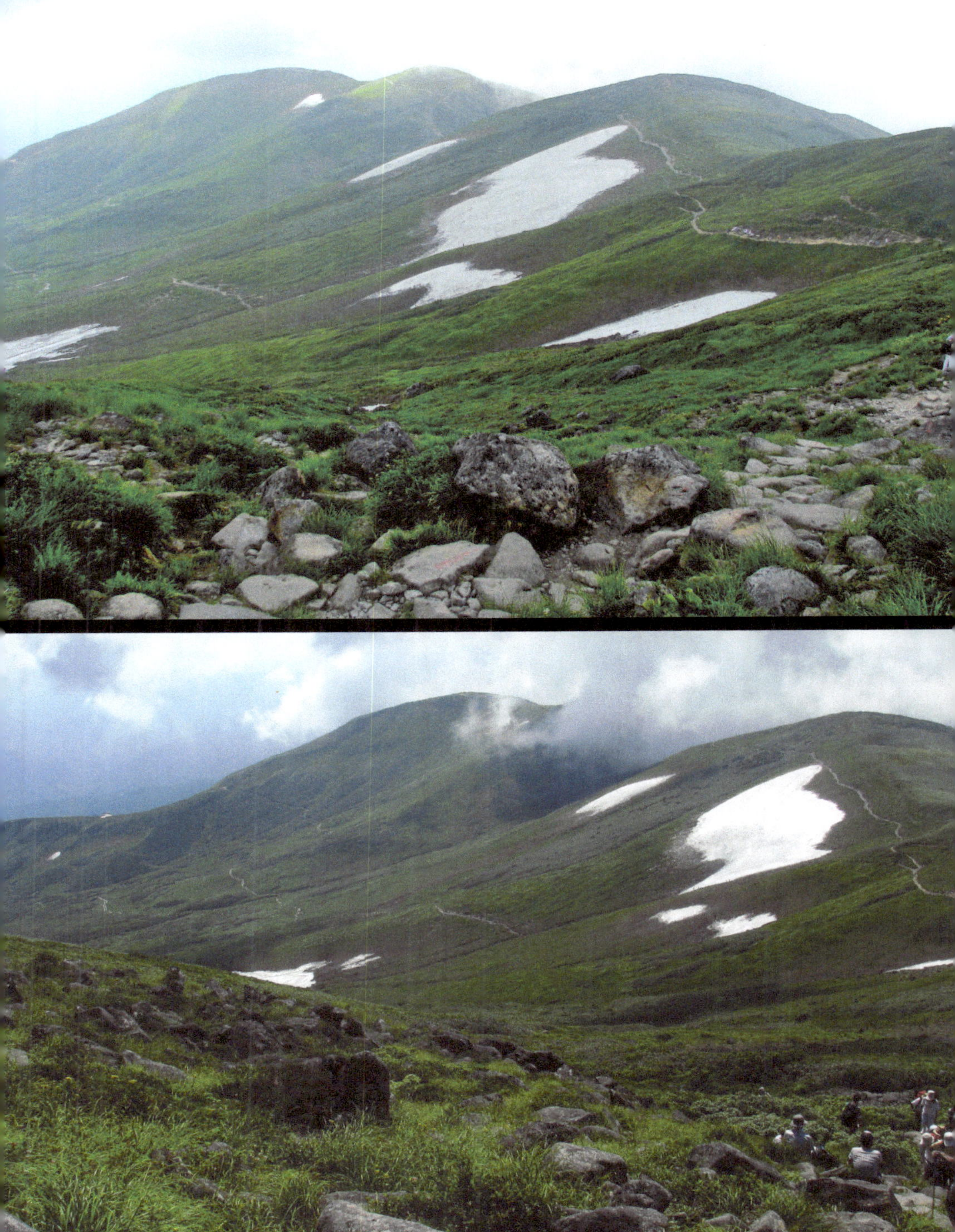

Then, after you arrive at the top of this slope you suddenly see the summit hut! This is the hut which offers accommodation. In this photo, taken on August 12, 2008 at 2:47 PM it is probably difficult for you to know that we are in the clouds. The photo gives the impression that the hut is right at the very summit of the mountain and that from here it is down on all sides. Well, be patient and we'll show you another photo which was taken after the clouds parted for us. The clouds continued to come and go on this date.

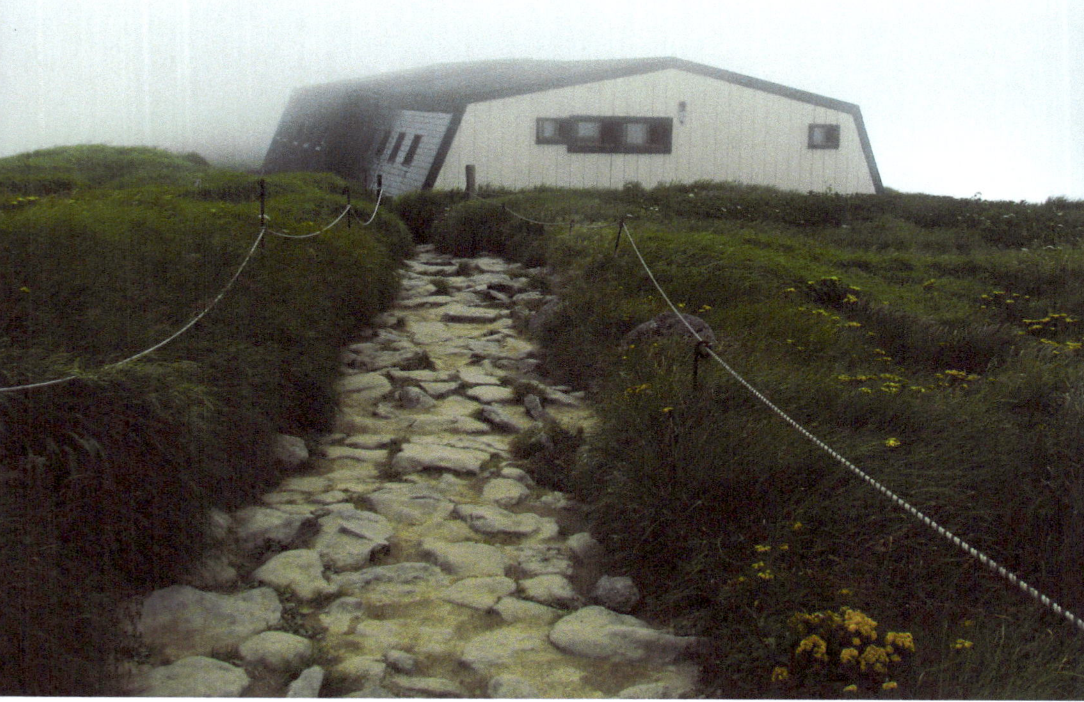

The next photo, on the facing page, taken on the same date, but forty-nine minutes later – at 3:36 PM – is a shot which was taken from a spot very close to the same as the above photo. In this photo you can see that the mountain does not drop off on all sides from the hut, as one would think from the above photo. As you can see, there is a Buddhist Shrine at the very summit of the mountain.

You can enter this shrine for a fee of ¥500 and one of the monks will say some prayers and go through a purification ritual for you. We entered the shrine in 2008 – the first time we were here – but we did not enter it in 2011.

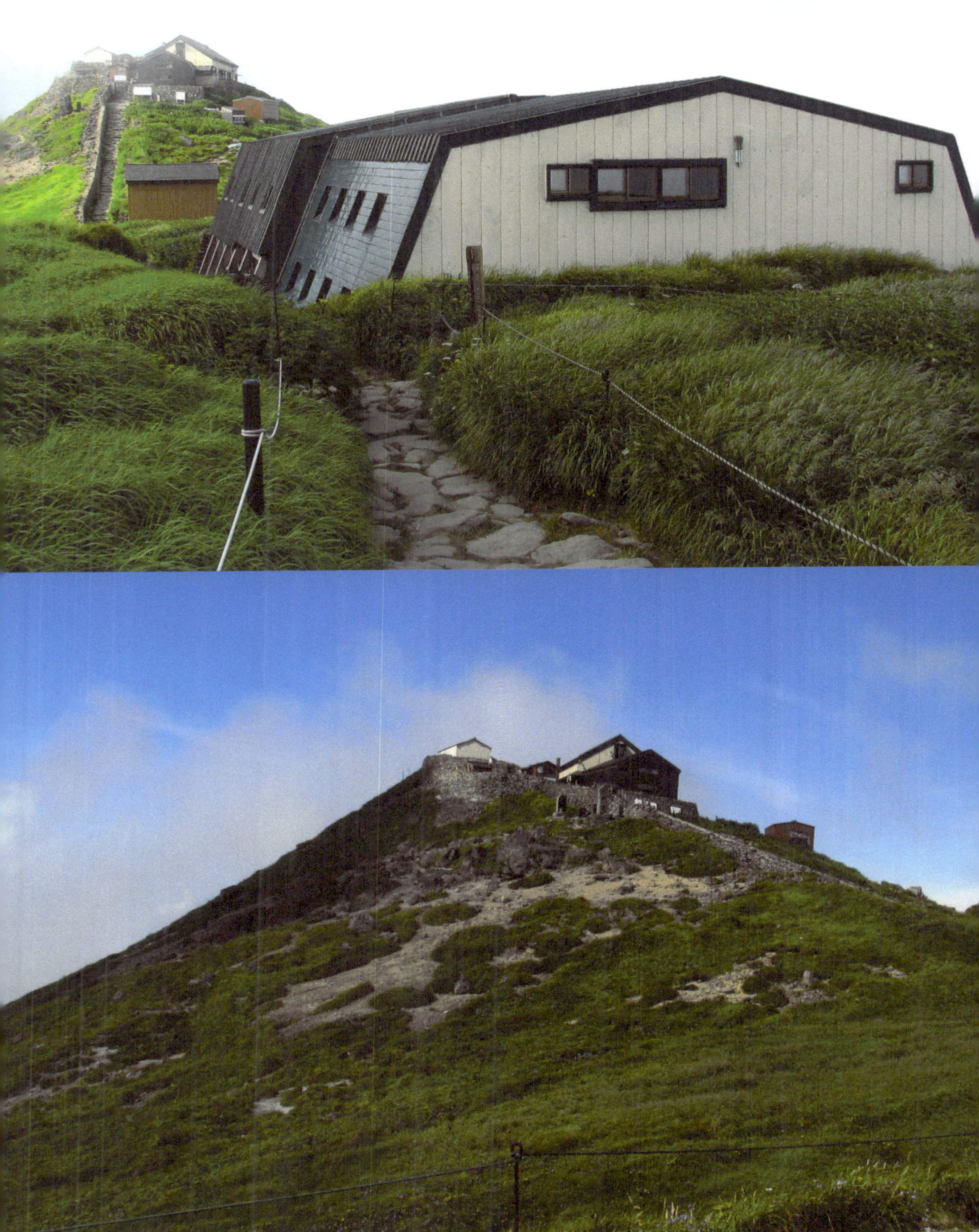

The previous photo was taken on August 6, 2011 at 3:08 PM from a scenic overlook which is only about a two minute walk from the hut. After drinking some water and purchasing a cold beer and a snack at the hut we walked out here to enjoy our cold and very refreshing can of beer. This photo shows the shrine area at the summit of the mountain in full sun and at maximum beauty, with all of the green vegetation and the blue sky.

The following photo was also taken on August 6, 2011, but it was taken at 3:21 PM, a mere thirteen minutes after the one just previous. You can easily discern that it is still sunny, but at this moment a thin cloud is passing by. Amazingly rapid change in the weather, eh!

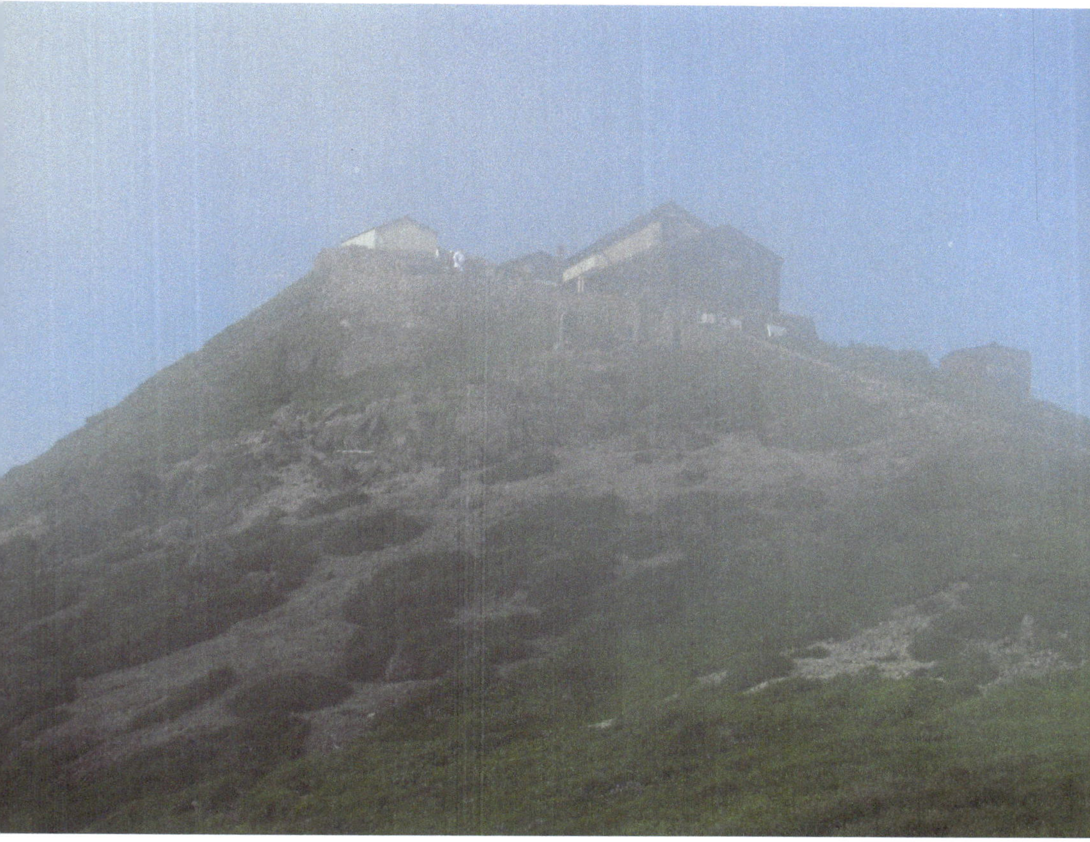

Now, we have no more photos until it is approaching sunset time. And the next photo, a flower photo, is included to show you the great abundance of wildflowers which you will see here. If you don't appreciate wildflowers then please just ignore it. It is quite amazing though.

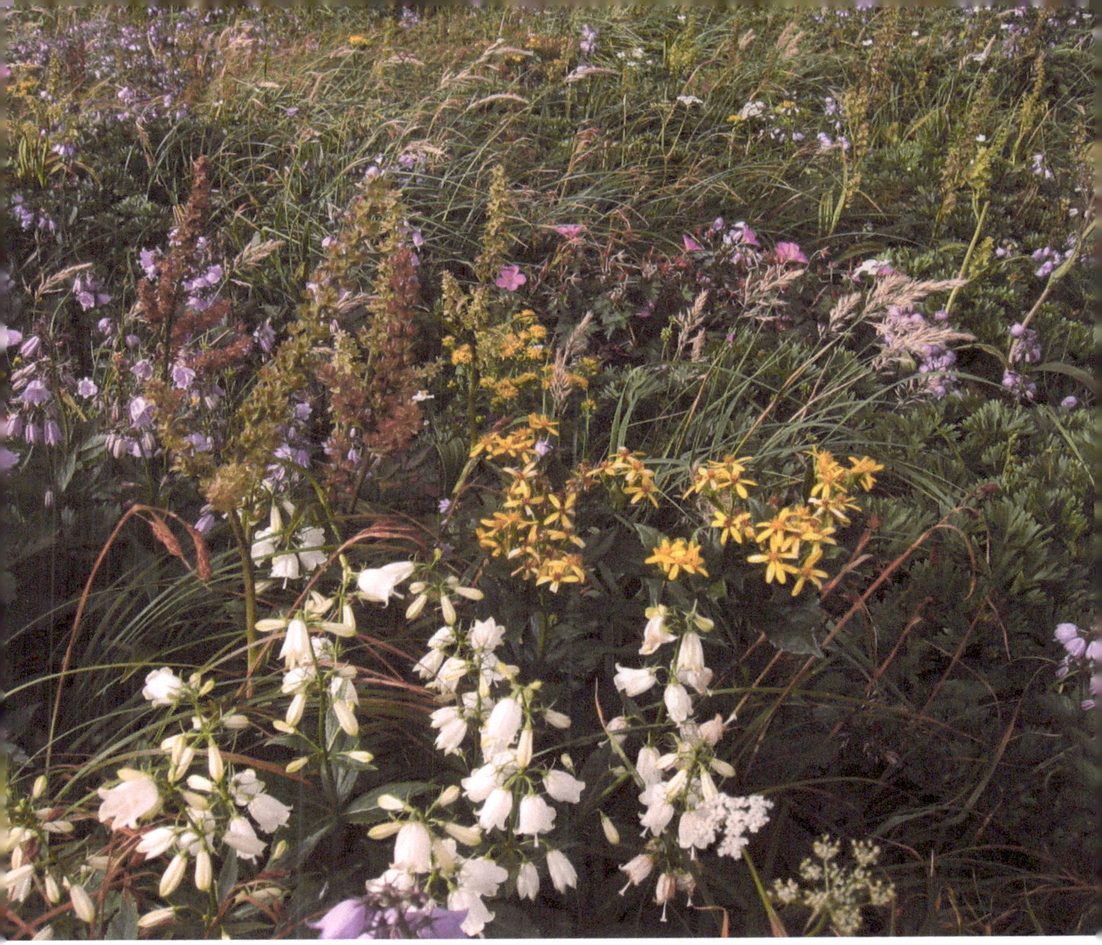

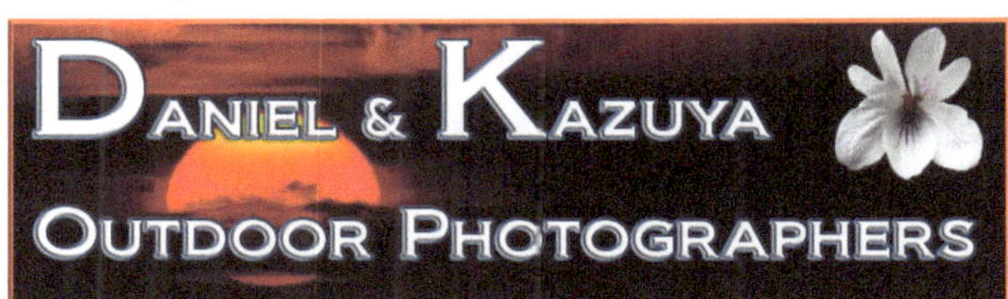

The next two photos, both taken on our 2008 climb of this mountain, show the setting sun. We experienced the most incredible sunset on this, the 12th of August, 2008. We probably shot one hundred or more photos of this sunset.

The upper photo on the following page was shot at 6:40 PM and the lower one was shot at 6:41 PM. It nearly looks like the sun is setting through oil or something. If you are very astute you might notice that the lower photo looks, somehow, familiar — the reason is because a small cropped out portion of that photo is part of what makes up our logo, which you saw on the first page of this book, which you see on all of our website pages and which is included immediately below to refresh your memory.

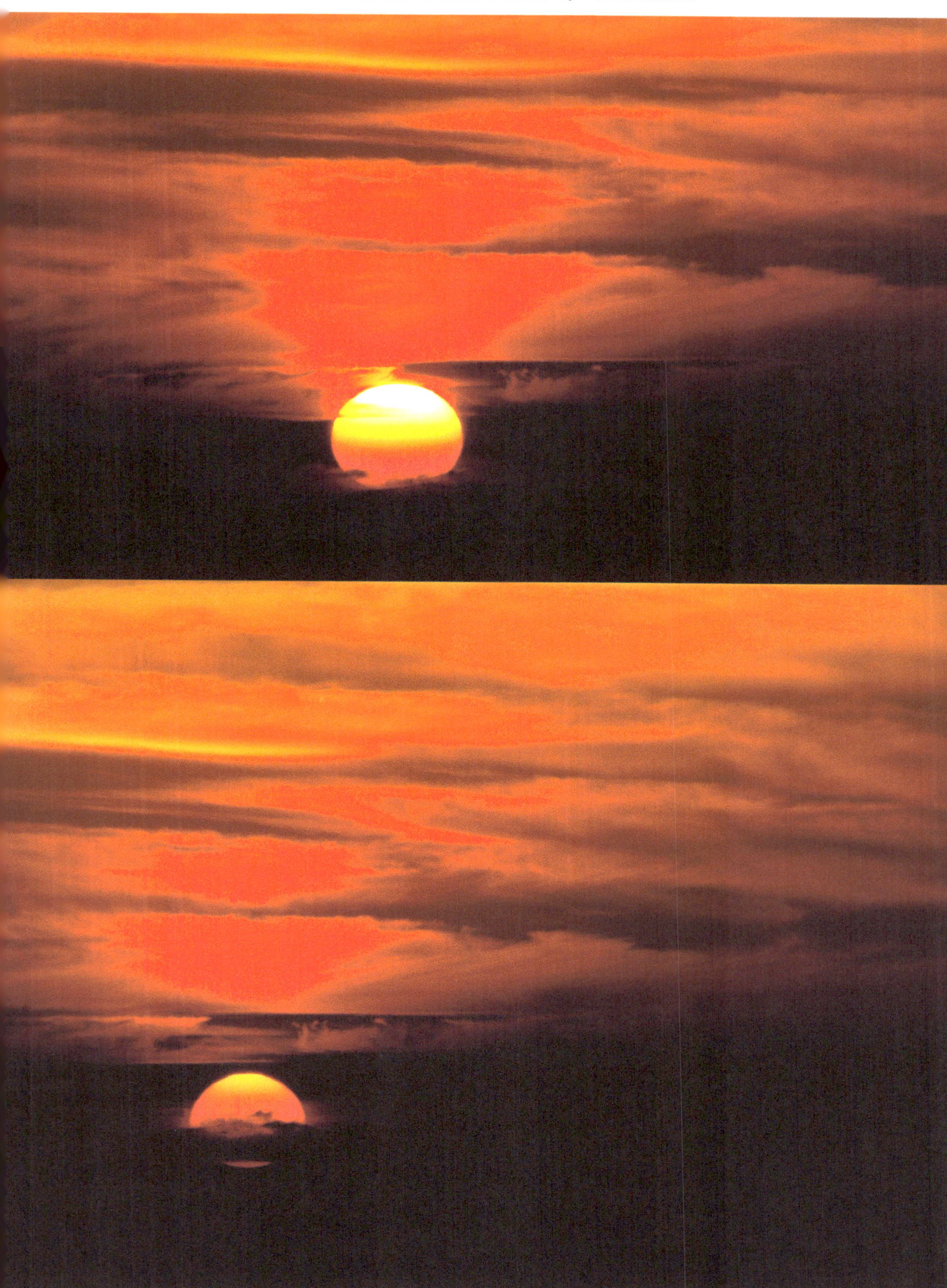

The following photo shows a scene which was shot during the sunset period when we climbed this mountain in 2011. It was shot on August 6, 2011 at 6:46 PM and shows that a sea of clouds has rolled in below us. The people who live down in the valley below are now 100% covered by clouds. A very beautiful photo, no?

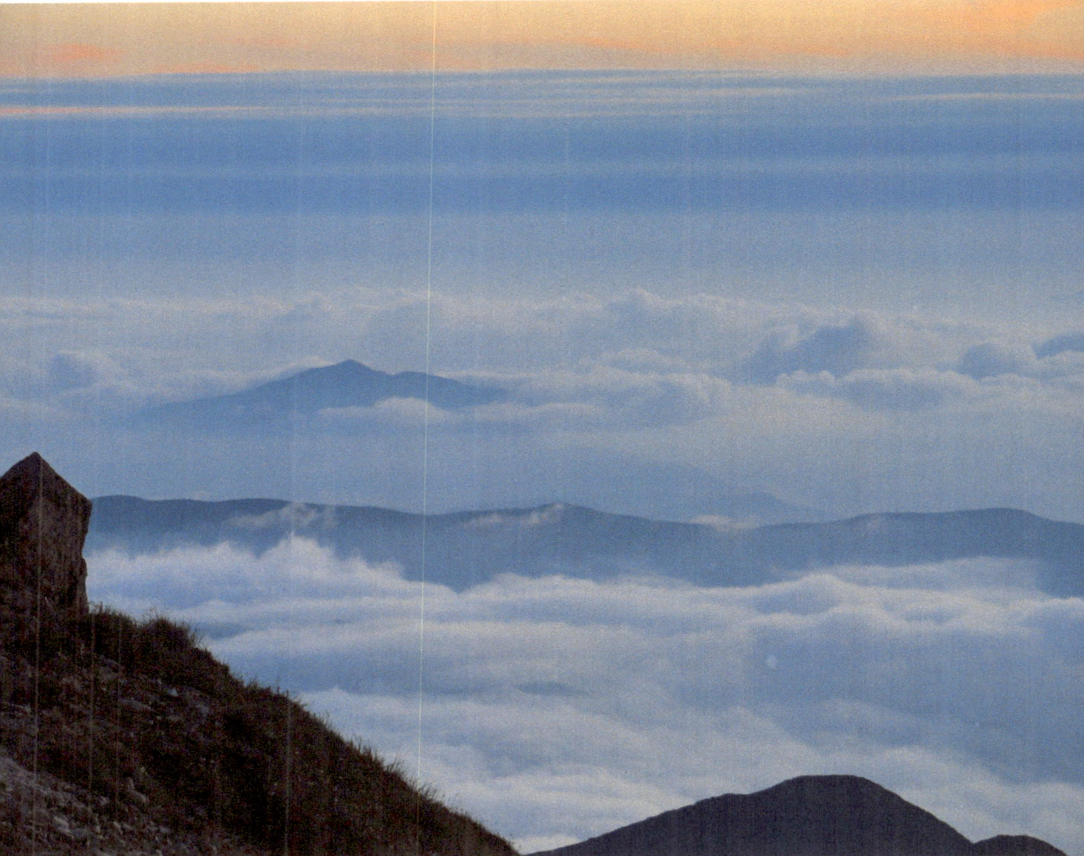

The next photo was also taken on August 6, 2011, which was only four minutes after the one just above. It shows some very interesting colors. During the sunset time on this climb we were only given fleeting glimpses of the sun itself and in this photo the bright area at the bottom left corner is where the sun is hiding behind the clouds.

Okay, that ends the ascent of Mt. Gassan and it's now time for dinner in the hut and then shortly after that it till be time to sleep. Now, we have to get up early in the morning, catch some sunrise photos, eat breakfast in the hut and then pack up and make our descent. We have descended, both in 2008 and also in 2011 via the trail to the north from the summit – the one which is marked with the 6. annotation on the map. But, before we descend, let's take some sunrise time photos.

The upper photo on the facing page was taken at 4:42 AM on August 13, 2008, it is, obviously before sunrise. The lower photo was taken at 4:44 AM, just two minutes later. We will not catch our first glimpse of the sun until about 4:50 AM. Don't worry, we'll also show you one of those photos.

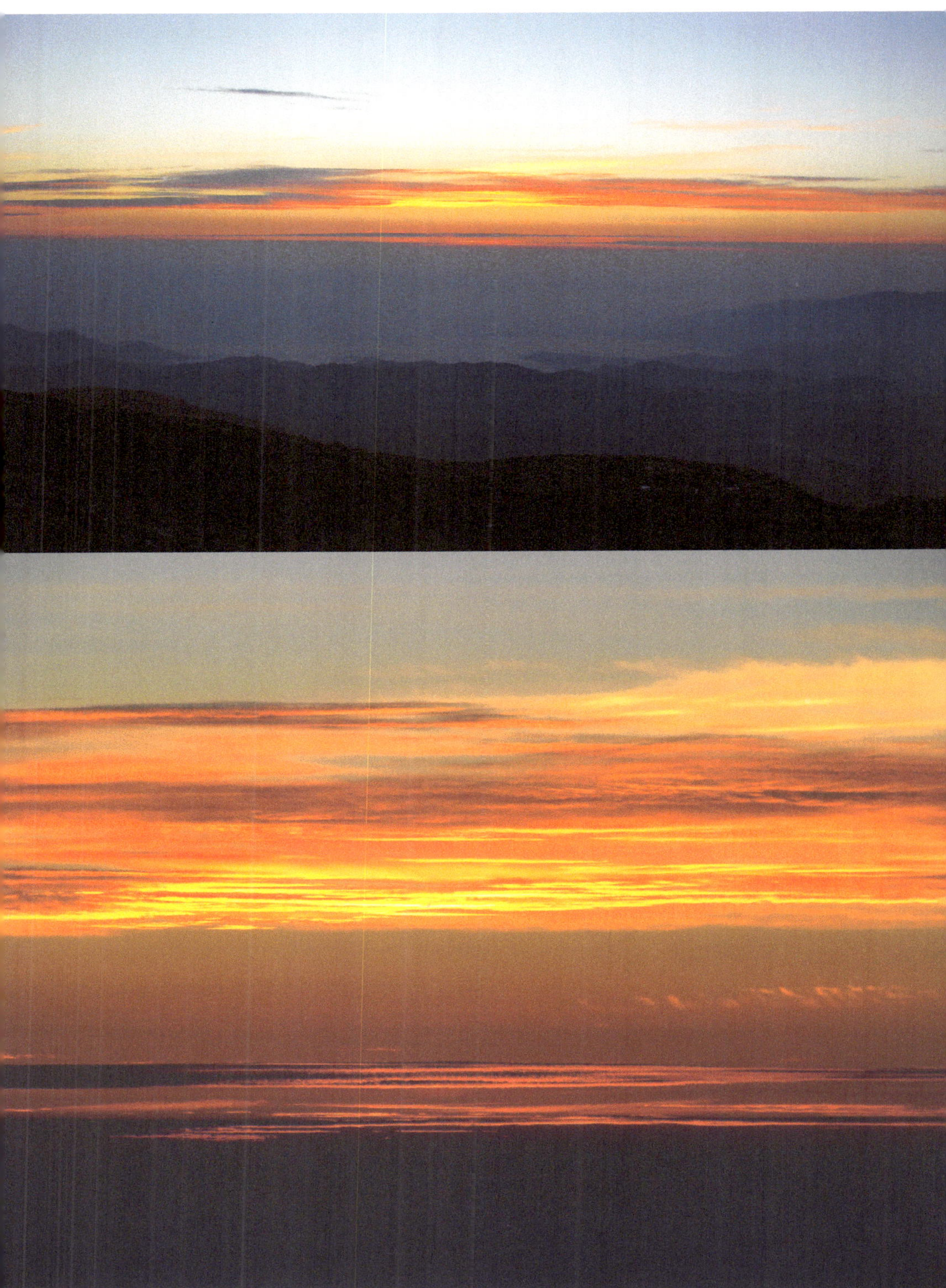

Here, just below is that photo which we promised just above — the one where you can actually see the sun rising. The time is now 4:52 AM, August 13th, 2008.

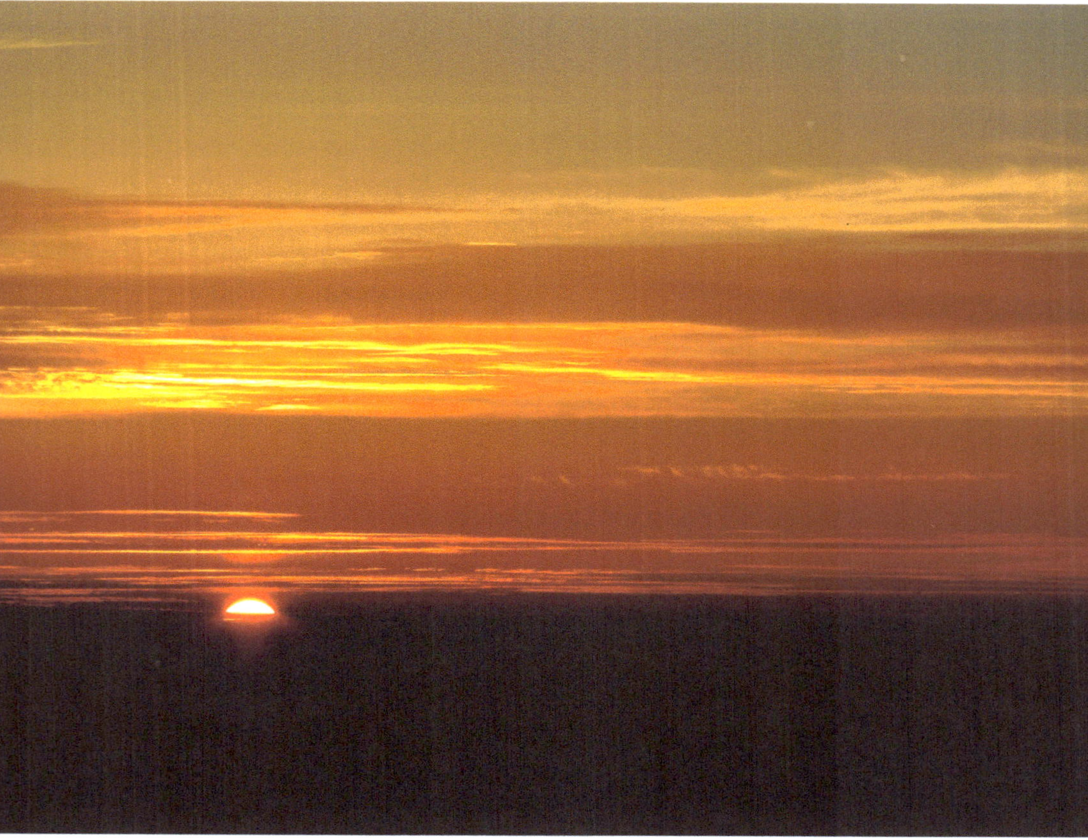

The following photo, on the facing page, shows the sun after it has fully risen above the horizon, but not 100% risen above the cloud layer. It was shot at 4:56 AM. There is again a sea of clouds down in the valley below us. It is a sure thing that the people who live down there are not seeing the sun as it rises. They are probably wondering, in fact, if they are going to get rained upon today! If we recall correctly, they did not get rained upon.

The lower photo on the facing page is included to show you the orange-red coloration on everything we see due to this sunrise. You'll notice it on the small snowfield, the white flowers, the seedheads of the grass — literally everything.

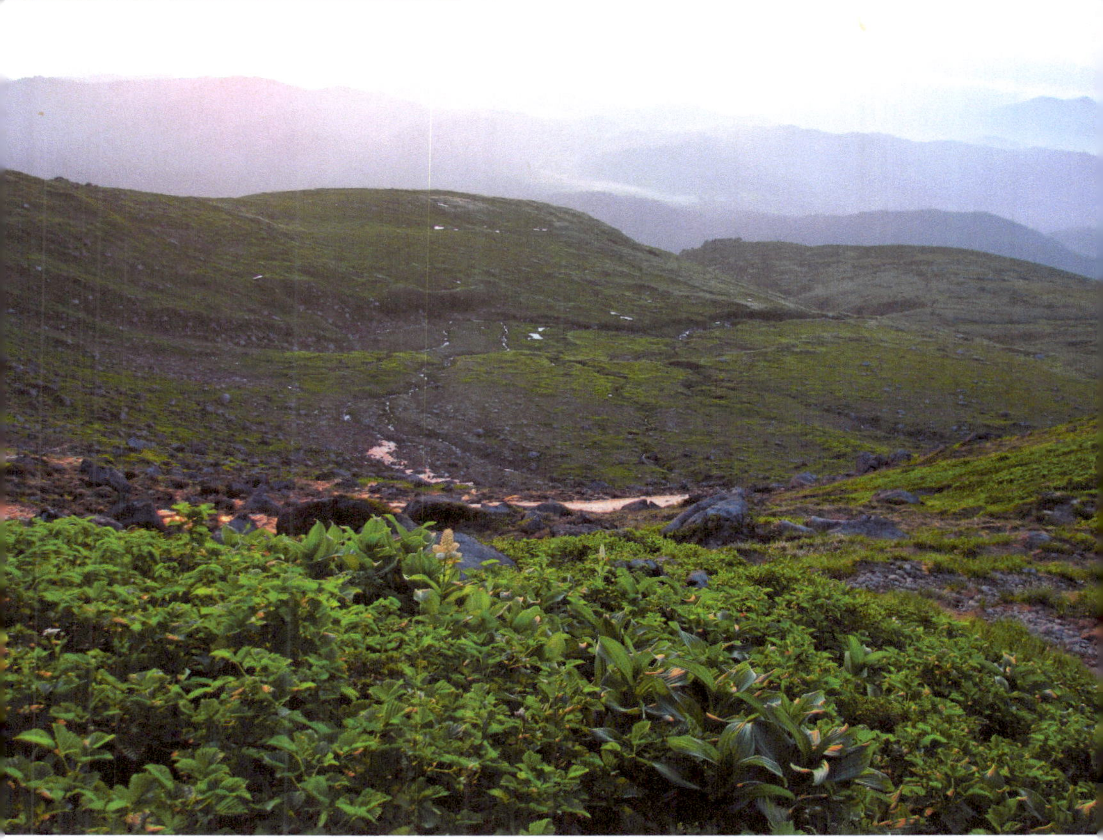

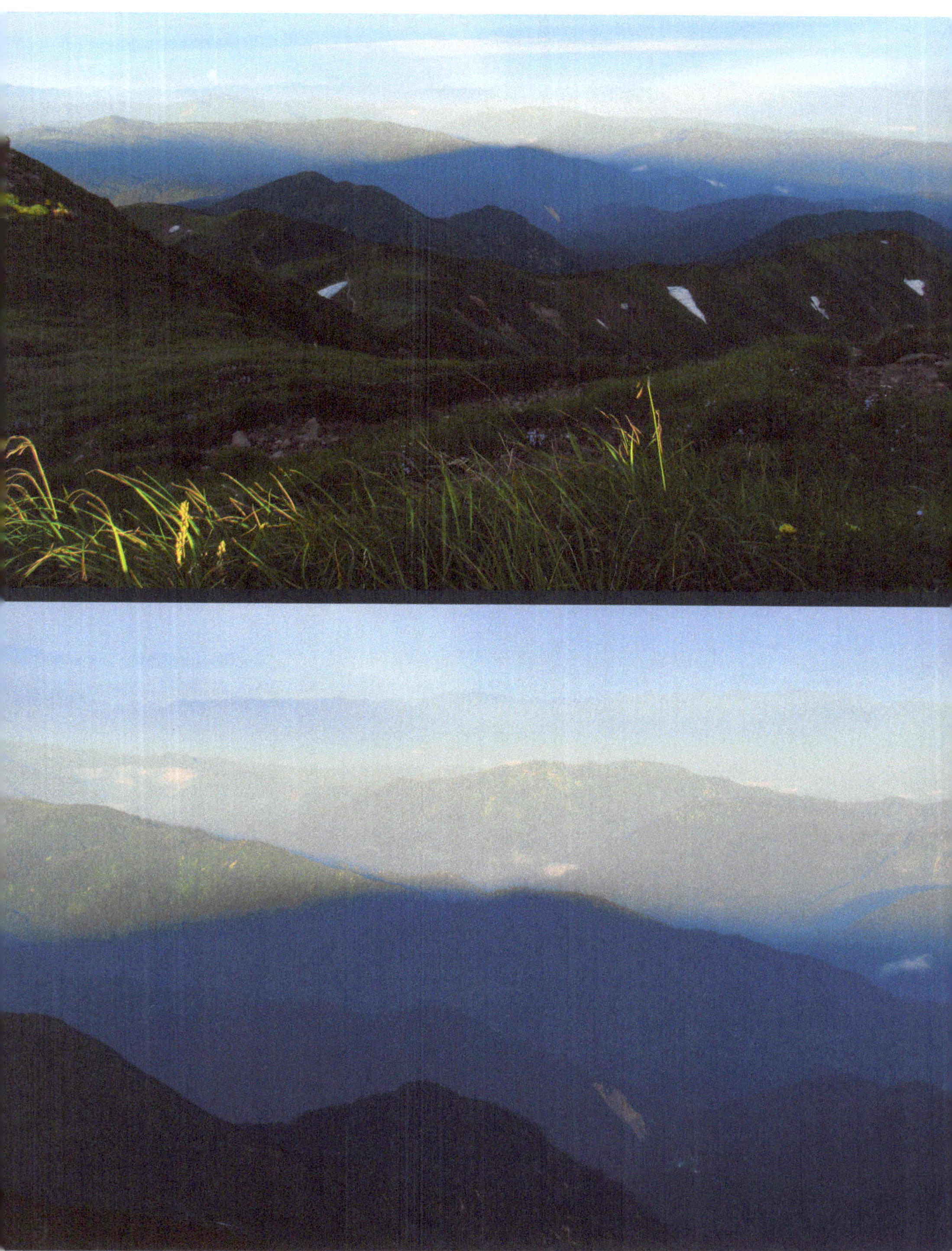

The two photos on the facing page are included to show you the shadow of this mountain. They were both shot at 5:20 AM. The lower photo is a zoomed version of the upper photo. If you read Volume 2 of this series of books you were given the opportunity to see the shadow of Mt. Chokai on the Sea of Japan. This shadow is not as amazing as that, but it's always at least somewhat amazing to see the shadow of a mountain which you are at the top of. We have seen this from the tops of several mountains we have climbed and we have never been able to stop ourselves from taking some photos of it.

The photo just below gives you a final look at the hut where we stayed – and where you can also stay if you so desire. This was taken as we hiked north and we were just about right beside the small shrine which you have seen in previous photos. It was taken at 5:23 AM on August 7, during our 2011 descent.

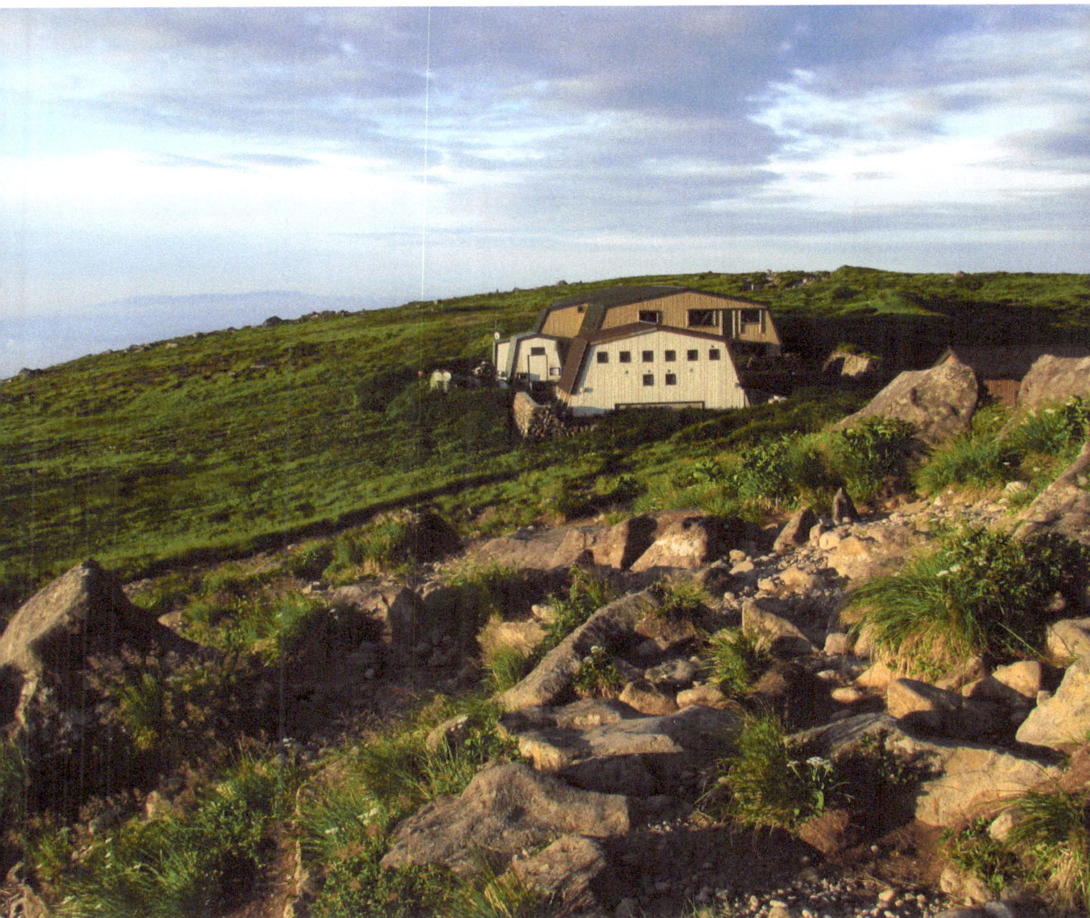

The following photo was taken on August 7, 2011 at 5:25 AM and it is interesting for the fog in the various valleys which you can see. You should also note the abundance of small ponds down on the plateau immediately below us. Each of those blue spots is a pond.

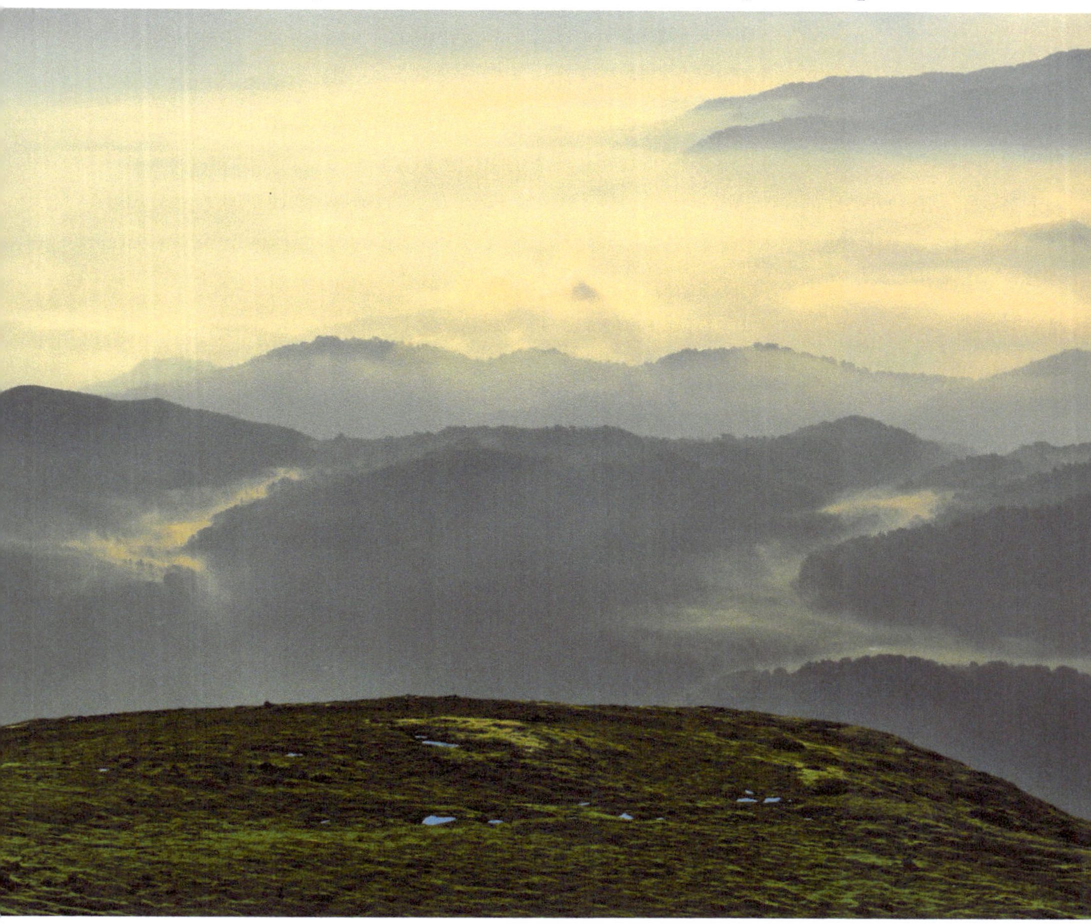

In the upper photo on the facing page you can see Kazuya hiking on the boardwalk which is just to the north of the shrine. In fact, that green grassy knoll on the right side of the photo hides the shrine. That means that the photo was taken looking back to the south.

The lower photo on the facing page shows a scenic shot taken from approximately the same location, however, it was shot looking to the north. The mountain far off in the distance is Mt. Chokai, which was the subject of Volume 2 in this series of books.

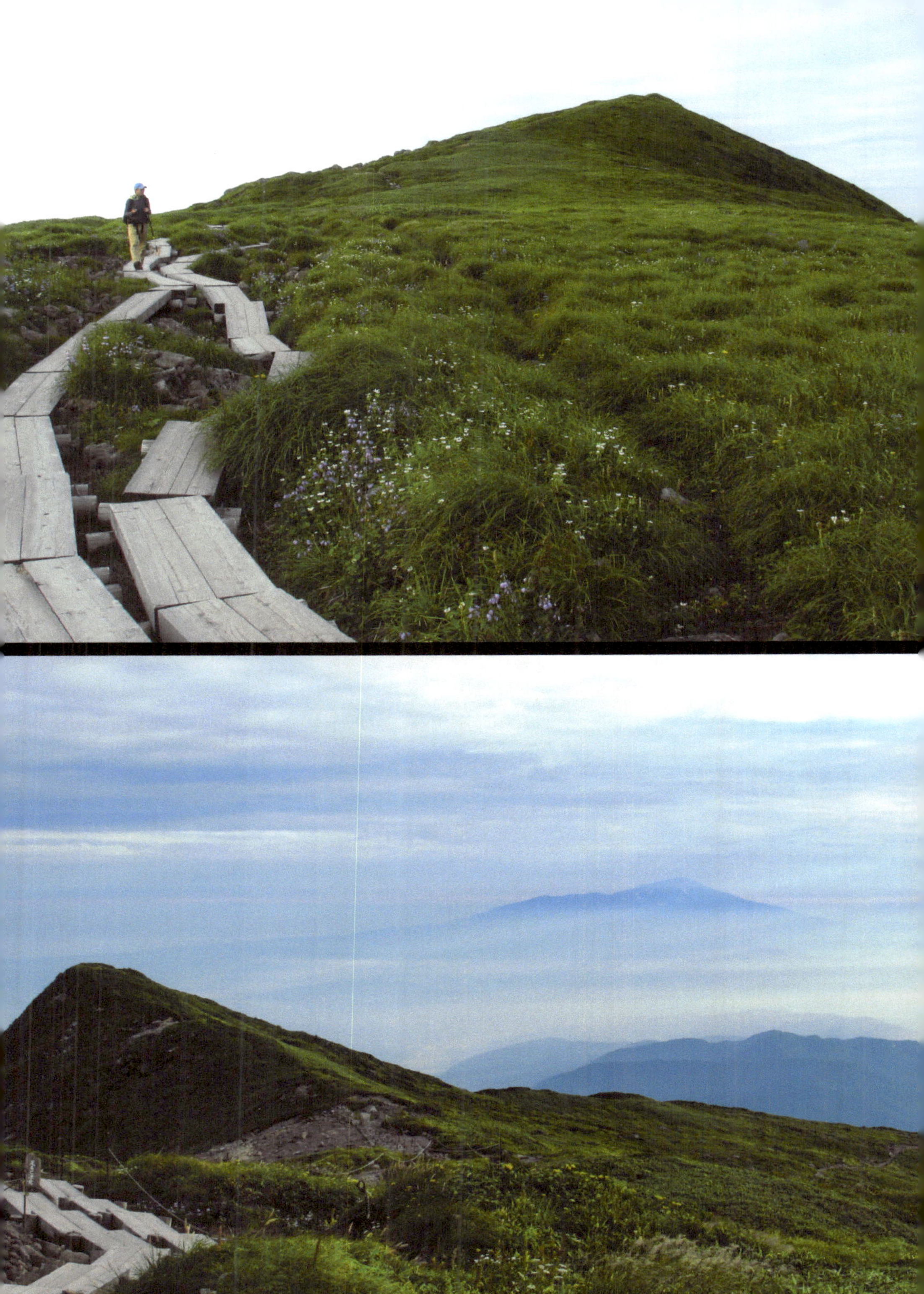

Now let's have one shot zoomed in to Mt. Chokai. This shot below was taken on August 7, 2011 at 5:49 AM. It is certainly not the best possible photo, but considering that the distance between the two mountains is at least 130 km (81 miles), it's not really a terrible photo!

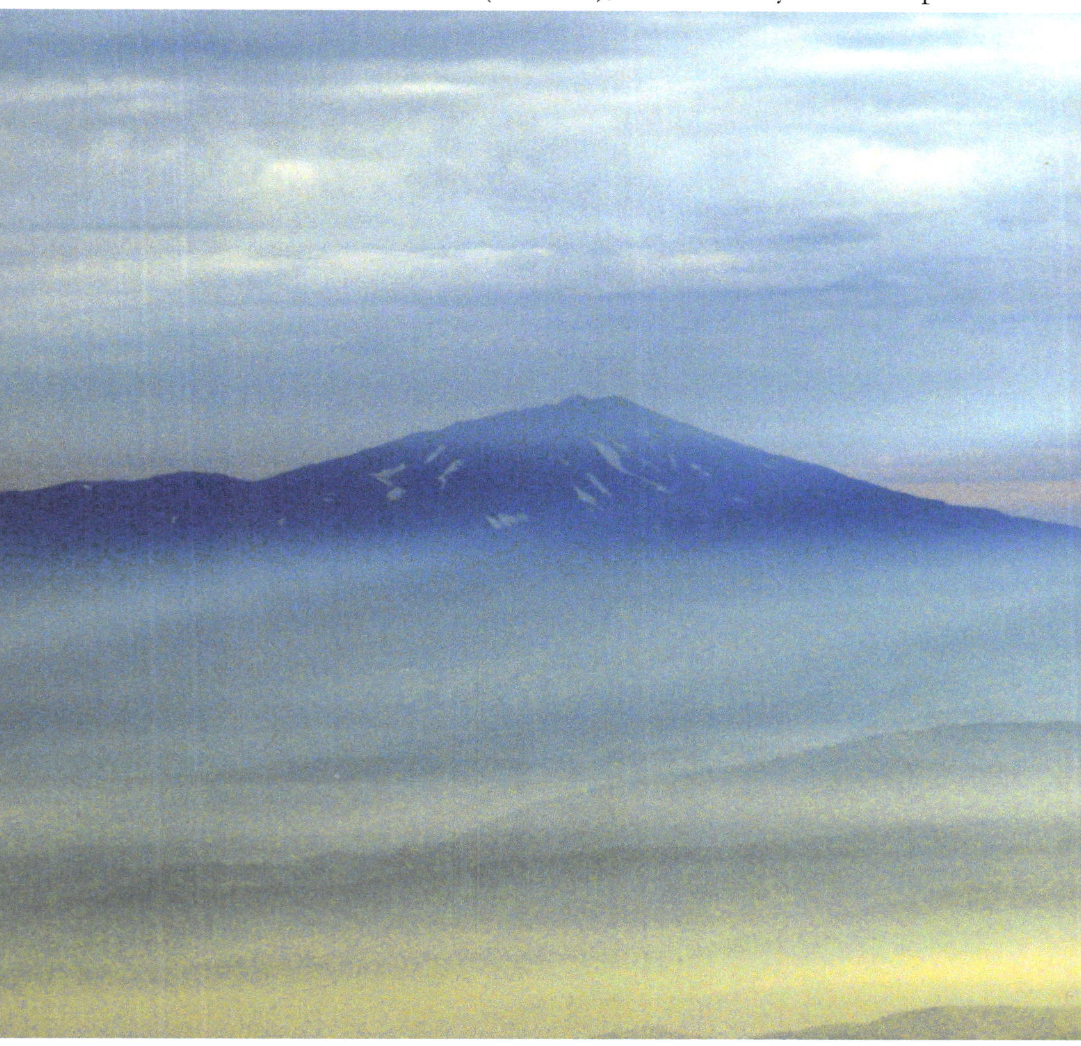

The following two photos, on the facing page, both show some very interesting clouds, sun rays and colors. They were both shot on August 7, 2011 at 5:55 AM.. The upper image shows the approximate area which is outlined in the lower image. Please also note the abundance of wildflowers in the immediate foreground in the lower photo.

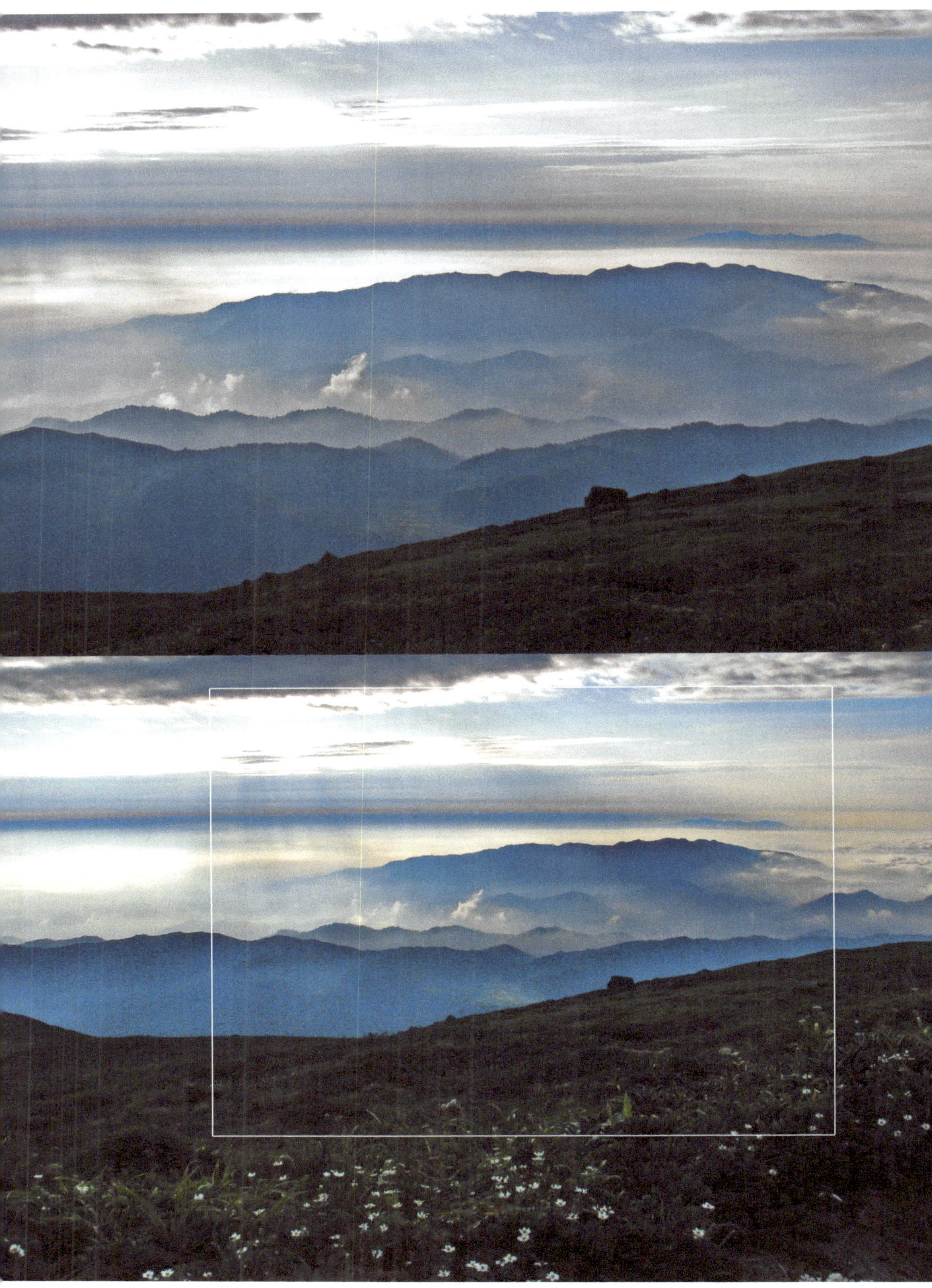

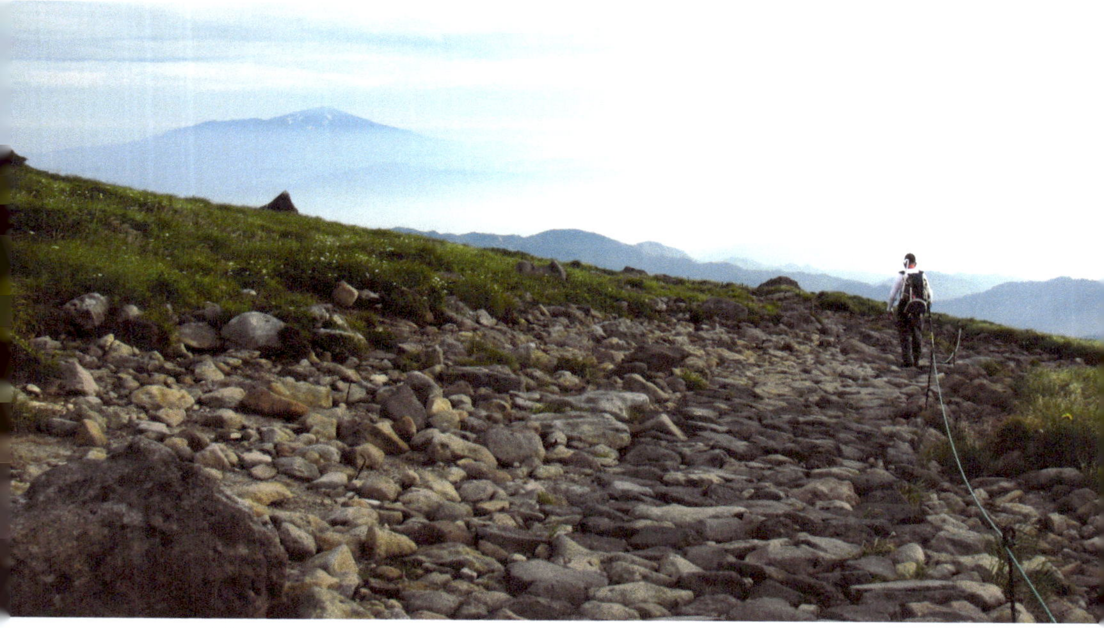

  This photo shows me on the trail, which is again rock and not as easy to walk on as it may appear. This shot was taken on that long stretch of trail between the 5. and 6. annotations on the map. Note that you can once again see Mt. Chokai off in the distance in this photo.

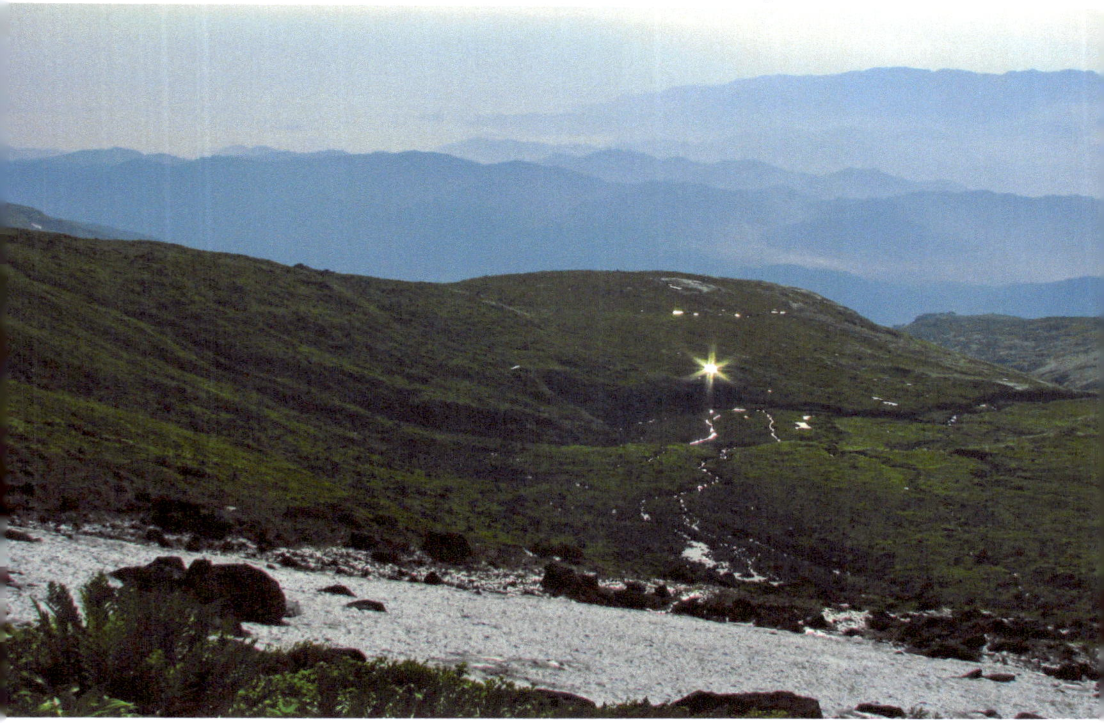

The lower photo on the facing page is both interesting and also strange. It was taken at 6:19 AM on August 13, 2008 as we were descending the mountain and we looked down and saw this diamond shining in our eyes. Of course it is a small pond which just happened to be reflecting the sun in such a way so that we had this amazing view. Naturally, it disappeared about one minute later. Here is one more photo of this amazing phenomenon.

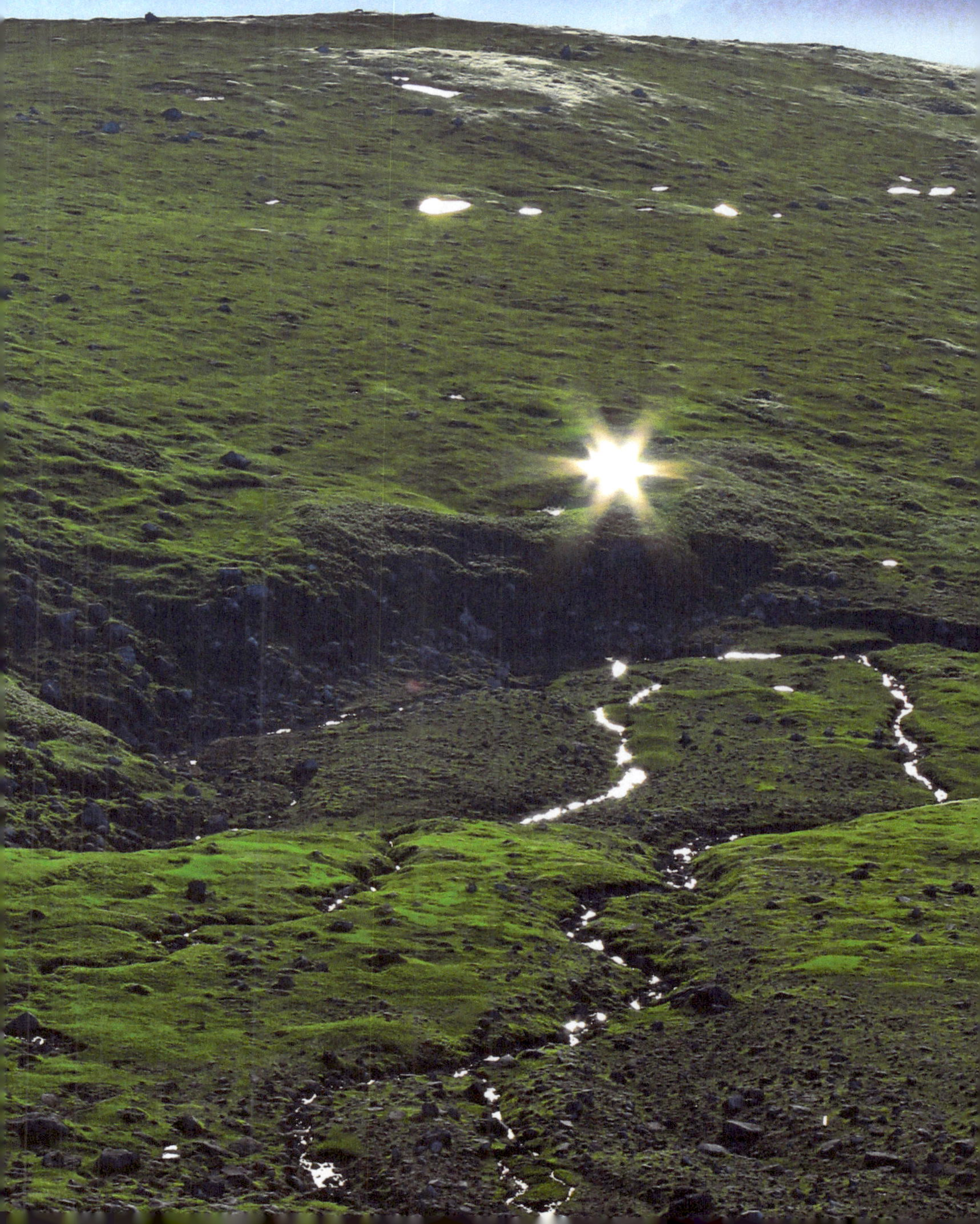

This photo shows the hut which is indicated by the 6. annotation on the map back on page 13. It was taken from very close to the point which shows 1828 as the elevation on the map（オモワシ山）(Omowashi-yama). In this photo the weather and sky is still mostly haze free and you can still see Mt. Chokai off in the distance. It was taken on August 13, 2008 at 7:17 AM.

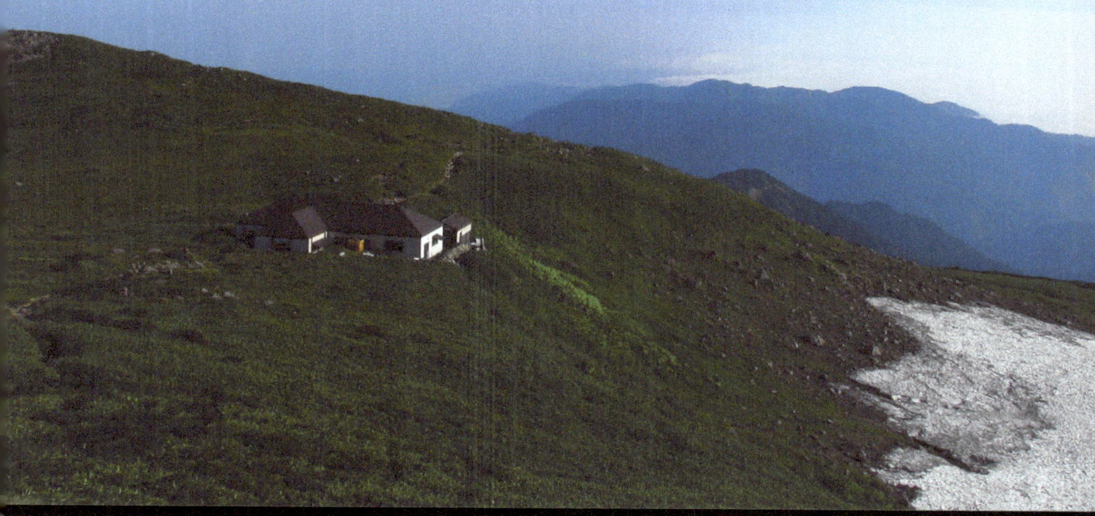

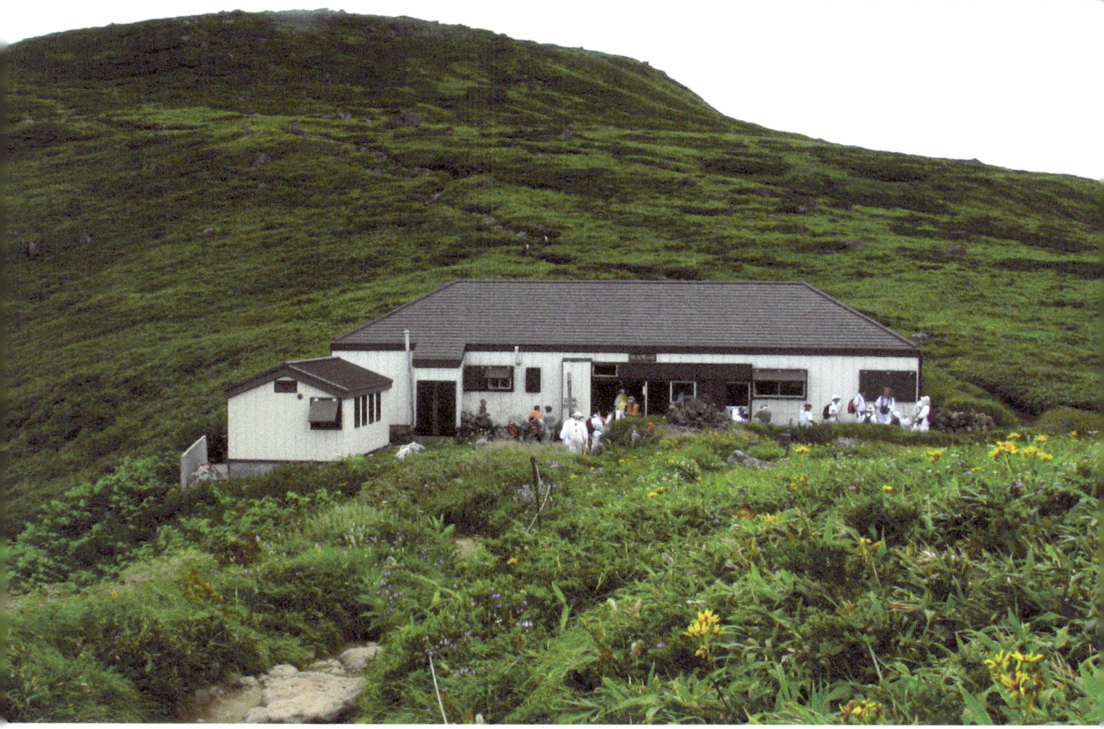

The lower photo on the facing page, taken during our 2011 descent, shows the same hut as the photo above it. This photo is included to show the group of white-clothed pilgrims hiking to or from the summit. We mentioned earlier that due to the fact that this is a sacred mountain these groups can often be seen. Their garb is truly amazing – they are TOTALLY dressed in white, they even purchase white backpacks somewhere for these pilgrimages. We have no idea where white backpacks can be found, possibly at the Buddhist clothing stores, or maybe special items for winter camouflage, who knows?

The following two photos show the lower hut, marked with the 7. annotation on the map. As you can see on the map, there are several ponds around this hut. The first photo, with the sunny blue sky was taken on August 13, 2008 at 8:18 AM.

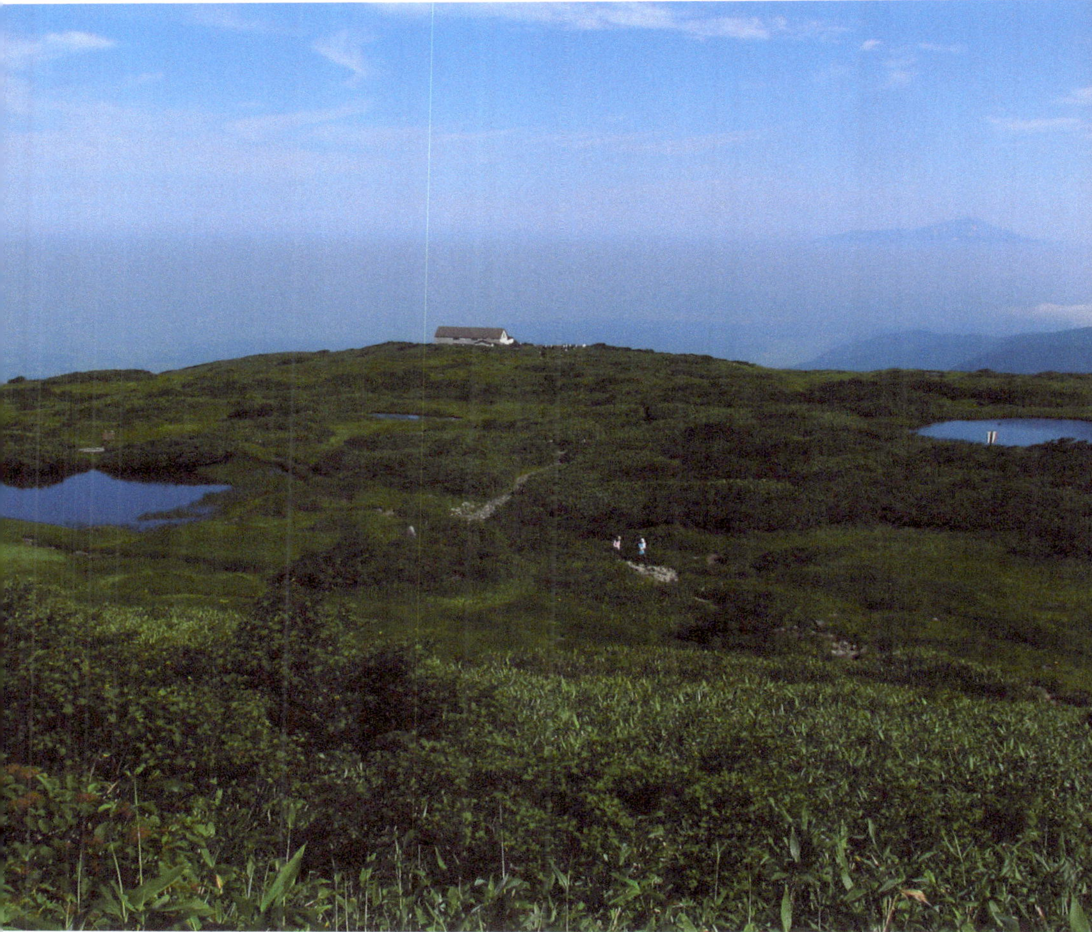

This next photo, which shows virtually the same scene as the previous photo, is included for two reasons. First, it is included to show the difference in the weather we had during our two descents of this mountain. This photo was taken on August 7, 2011 at 8:08 AM. Note that although it was cloudier in 2011, we could actually see Mt. Chokai better. The second reason this next photo is included is to show you another group of white-clothed pilgrims, apparently hiking towards the summit. We often saw these groups higher on the mountain also, but for some reason we never took any photos of them until we reached this point.

You'll note on the map (page 13) that there is one more annotation – 8. – which is used to mark the end of the descent along the trail and the parking lot where you can catch a bus to take you to a few different destinations. At this point we are not far from this bus stop and parking lot.

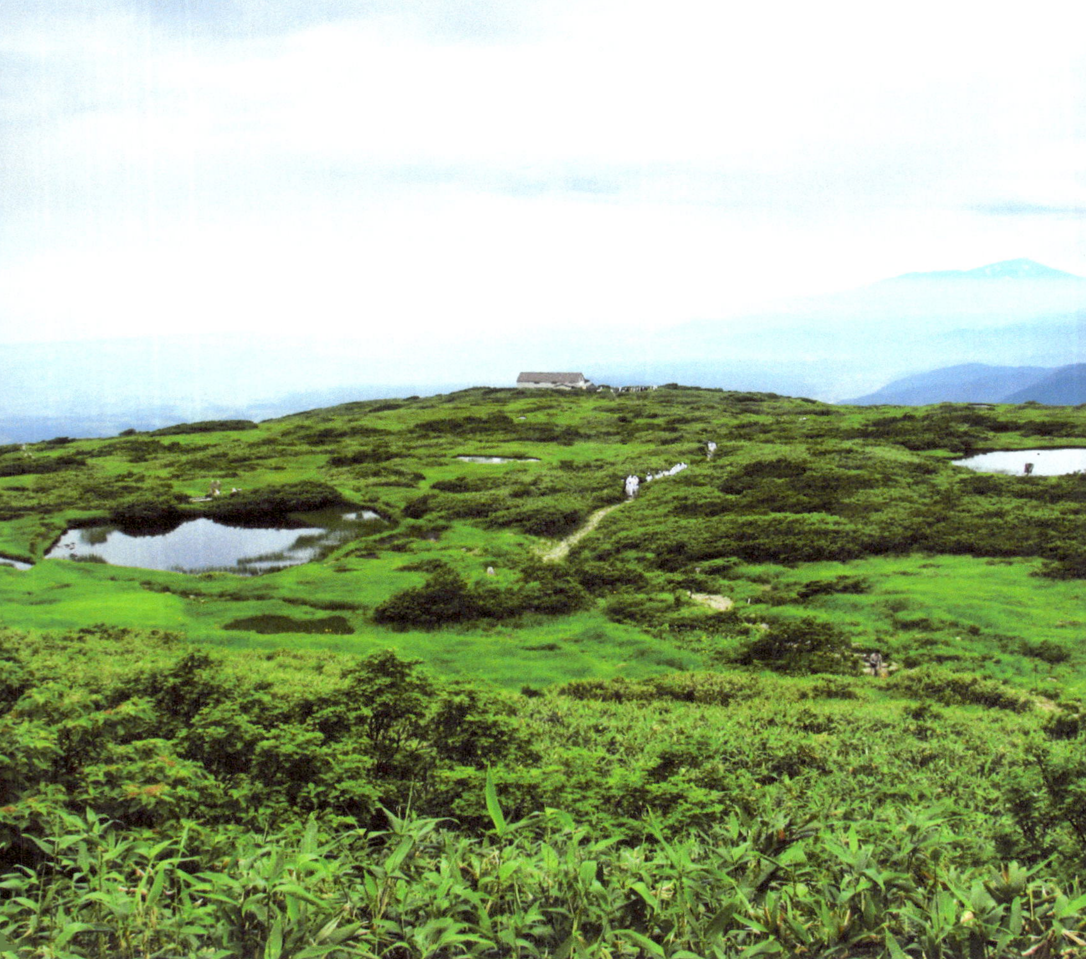

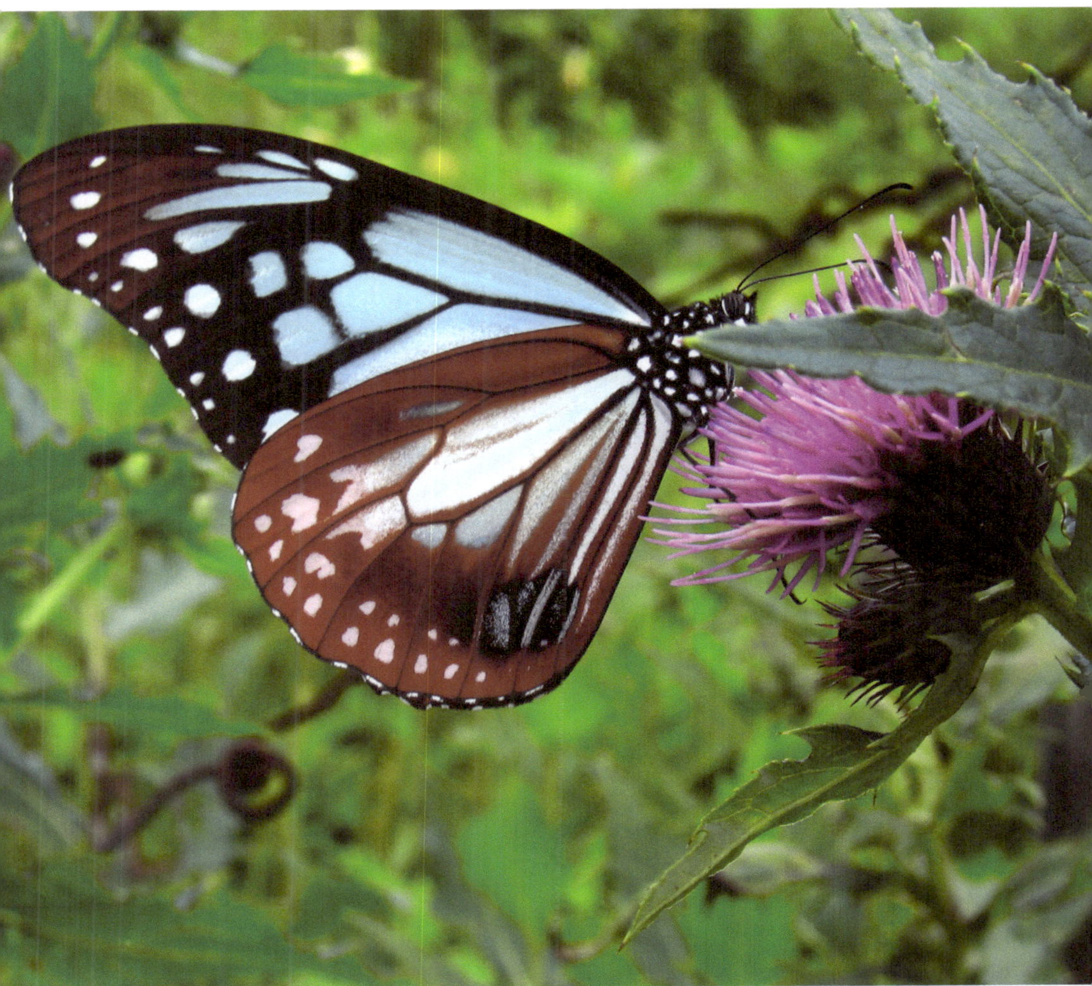

This photo immediately above just could not be omitted. It is just too amazingly beautiful. It was taken near the ponds which you saw above and shows a beautifully colored butterfly sitting on a thistle.

As stated near the start of this chapter – Mt. Gassan is the highest peak in the Dewa Sanzan trio of sacred mountains. Dewa Sanzan means "Three Mountains of Dewa" and indeed comprises the three sacred mountains of Mt. Hagurosan (羽黒山), Mt. Gassan (月山) and Mt. Yudonosan (湯殿山), clustered together in the ancient province of Dewa (modern-day Yamagata Prefecture). In light of this, it is not surprising that one of the destinations one can decide to go to from the parking lot and bus stop at the 8. annotation is the Mt. Hagurosan Shrine area. From the bus stop there, one can choose more destinations to travel to than one can from the Mt. Gassan bus stop (annotation 8.). The Sanjin Gosaiden

Shrine, at the base of Mt. Hagurosan is very famous, and we visited that shrine after our 2011 descent. It is quite picturesque and very large and for this reason we have chosen two photos taken during our visit to it which we want to show you.

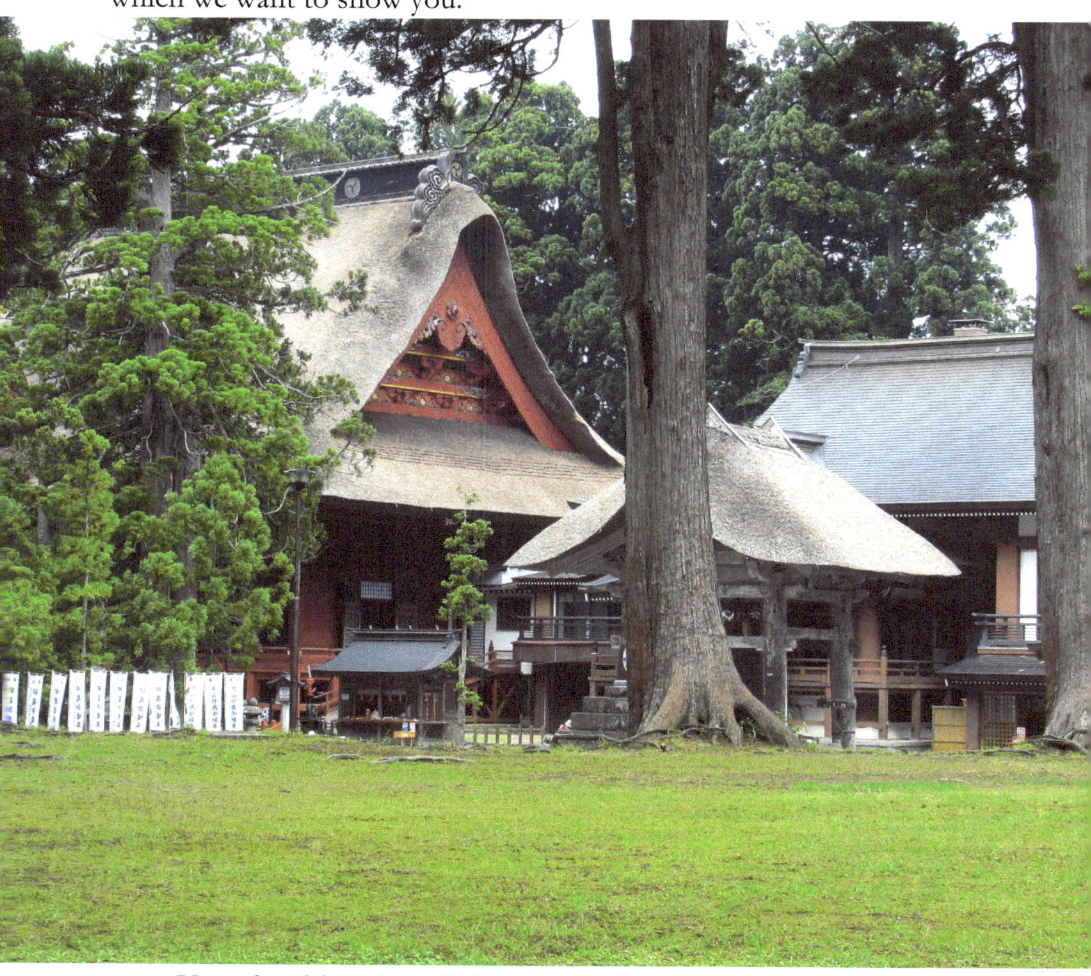

You should note well that these photos are not of the actual Hagurosan Shrine. These two photos are of the Sanjin Gosaiden Shrine. *This central shrine for Mt. Hagurosan, Mt. Gassan and Mt. Yudanosan is the most famous in Japan. Among the powerful sights at the shrine are the 2.1 meter thick thatched roof and the completely lacquered interior. It is definitely worth visiting* (text taken from an information sheet at the shrine). The following photo is another of Sanjin Gosaiden Shrine and it is a two-shot panorama – two portrait-mode shots! It gives a better impression of the size of this shrine than the above photo does and also shows some of the intricate beauty which one can see here. Of course you can also see the 2.1 m thick thatched roof.

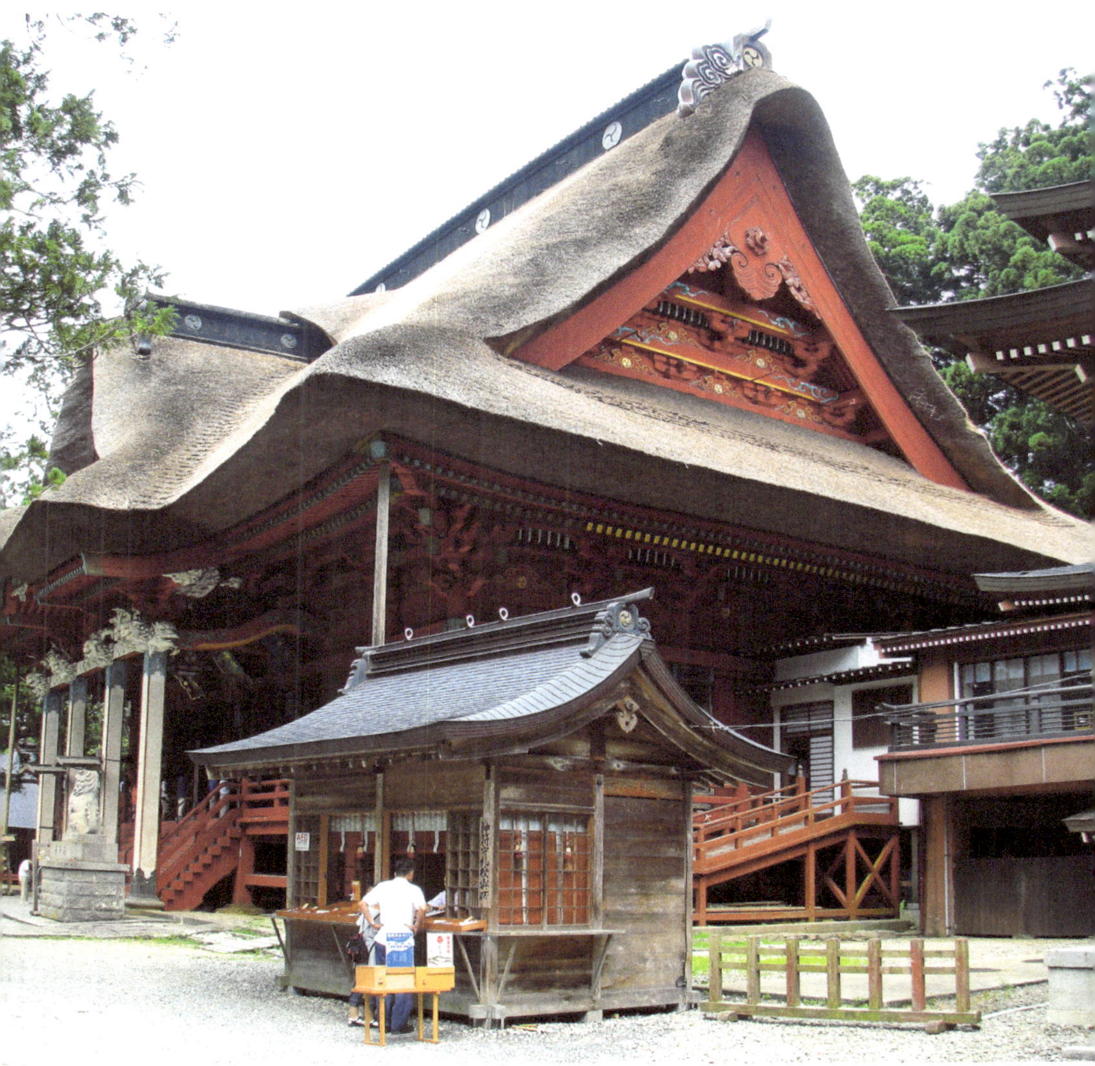

And that is the final photo for this, Volume 3, of this series of books on "Climbing a Few of Japan's 100 Famous Mountains". Please return for **Volume 4: Mt. Hakkoda & Mt. Zao**.

We sincerely hope that you are enjoying this series of books. If you would like any further information about any of these mountains there is a great abundance of it available on the internet.

If you want to e-mail me with specific questions you may do so through the link on my website, which is http://danwiz.com. I hope to maintain this site as long as I am alive.

THE END

ABOUT THE AUTHORS

Daniel Wieczorek was born in 1947 in Ionia, Michigan. He graduated from the University of Michigan with a B.S. in Forestry in 1969. He moved to Oregon to work in the field of forestry in 1971. That was followed by a move to Alaska in 1975, where he continued his career in forestry. After about a 14 year career in forestry, Daniel decided to do something different and he served as a Peace Corps Volunteer in The Philippines from 1985 – 1987. Upon completion of his Peace Corps service he returned to Alaska, where he attended the University of Alaska – Fairbanks and received an M.B.A. in 1991. This was followed by a move to South Korea in 1992, where Daniel taught English to Korean people wishing to improve their English Language skills. Daniel's next stop was in New York City, where he worked as temporary staff at Deutsche Bank from 1998 – 2001. He left NYC in March 2001 and moved on to his present home in Mitaka City, Tokyo, Japan. He is teaching English in Japan and at this time he's been teaching as a career for about 17 years. He has been hiking, climbing and doing photography since he was about 12 years old.

Kazuya Numazawa was born in 1979 in Shinjo in Yamagata Prefecture, Japan. He was raised in Funagata Town in Yamagata Prefecture. He graduated from Tokyo University in 2005. Since that time he has worked in several fields, but primarily in Cram Schools around the Mitaka Area.

Daniel and Kazuya met in 2001 and they have been hiking, mountain climbing and doing photography together since that time and generally enjoying life together.

NOTES

PHOTO CREDITS

Daniel's Photos:

Pages 9, 13, 14 bottom, 15, 16 top, 17, 18 all, 19, 20 all, 21, 22, 23 bottom, 24, 25, 26 top, 27 all, 28, 29, 30, 31 all, 32, 33 all, 34, 35 bottom, 36 all, 37, 38, 39 all, 40, 41 all, 42 all, 43, 44, 45 all, 46, 47 bottom, 48 bottom, 49, 50 all, 51, 52, 53, 54, 55.

Kazuya's Photos:

Pages 11, 12, 14 top, 18 top, 23 top, 26 bottom, 35 top, 47 top, 48 top.